"Gordon writes not as a professional biographer, or as a historian, but as a master of the story form, as a careful reader, as a woman attuned to power and longing and as a believer for whom God is a mystery but not a stranger. Gordon is perfectly matched with Joan of Arc, and the book she has written is both a compelling life story and a shrewd analysis of the mythical uses to which it has been put." —*The New York Times Book Review*

"Agree or disagree with Gordon's numerous insights and interpretations, she gives us Joan as she was, letting us fully appreciate why the Maid will grip our attention for all time." —*Forbes*

"Gordon's biographical meditation is a readable and substantive introduction to the life and meaning of this medieval heroine."
—*Christian Century*

"A bold 'biographical meditation' that persuades the skeptic to meditate on the inexplicable something Joan made happen, and keeps on happening, to this day." —*Kirkus Reviews*

"Gordon avoids the dramatic and approaches her brassy, devout and defiant subject with a thoughtful air. *Joan of Arc* is an engaging meditation on one of the West's most memorable figures."
—*Star-Telegram* (Fort Worth)

"A large part of the enjoyment here is the highly personal intelligence of Gordon's prose style, laying out the facts of Joan's career and her martyrdom, and considering their ramifications."
—*Seattle Post-Intelligencer*

ABOUT THE AUTHOR

Mary Gordon, McIntosh Professor of English at Barnard College, is the bestselling author of six novels, three collections of short stories, and two memoirs. She lives in New York City.

MARY GORDON

JOAN *of* ARC

A Life

A LIPPER™/ PENGUIN BOOK

PENGUIN BOOKS

Published by the Penguin Group

Penguin Group (USA) Inc., 375 Hudson Street, New York, New York 10014, U.S.A.

Penguin Group (Canada), 90 Eglinton Avenue East, Suite 700, Toronto,
Ontario, Canada M4P 2Y3 (a division of Pearson Penguin Canada Inc.)

Penguin Books Ltd, 80 Strand, London WC2R 0RL, England

Penguin Ireland, 25 St Stephen's Green, Dublin 2, Ireland (a division of Penguin Books Ltd)

Penguin Group (Australia), 250 Camberwell Road, Camberwell,
Victoria 3124, Australia (a division of Pearson Australia Group Pty Ltd)

Penguin Books India Pvt Ltd, 11 Community Centre, Panchsheel Park, New Delhi – 110 017, India

Penguin Group (NZ), 67 Apollo Drive, Rosedale, North Shore 0632,
New Zealand (a division of Pearson New Zealand Ltd)

Penguin Books (South Africa) (Pty) Ltd, 24 Sturdee Avenue,
Rosebank, Johannesburg 2196, South Africa

Penguin Books Ltd, Registered Offices: 80 Strand, London WC2R 0RL, England

First published in the United States of America by Viking Penguin,
a member of Penguin Putnam Inc. 2000
Published in Penguin Books 2008

1   3   5   7   9   10   8   6   4   2

Grateful acknowledgment is made for permission to reprint an excerpt from "Horae Canonicae"
from *W. H. Auden: Collected Poems* by W. H. Auden, edited by Edward Mendelson.
Copyright © 1955 by W. H. Auden. Reprinted by permission of Random House, Inc.

THE LIBRARY OF CONGRESS HAS CATALOGED THE HARDCOVER EDITION AS FOLLOWS:
Gordon, Mary.
Joan of Arc: a Penguin life/Mary Gordon.
p. cm.
ISBN 0-670-88537-1 (hc.)
ISBN 978-0-14-311397-3 (pbk.)
1. Joan, of Arc, Saint, 1412–1431.   2. Christian women saints—
France—Biography.   3. France—History—Charles VII, 1422–1461.
4. Charles VII, King of France, 1403–1461—Coronation.   I. Title.
DC103.G68 2000
944'.026'292—dc21   99-055678

Printed in the United States of America
Set in Centaur · Designed by Francesca Belanger

TO ANTOINETTE O'CEALLAIGH

who also grew up
thinking of Joan

Acknowledgments

THERE ARE over twenty thousand books about Joan of Arc in the Bibliotheque Nationale in Paris. This figure suggests the impossibility of reading even a substantial portion of what has been written about her. I am particularly indebted, therefore, to two excellent studies on Joan, Edward Lucie-Smith's and Marina Warner's, both entitled *Joan of Arc.*

Posterity has been fortunate that the records of Joan's trial have been preserved. The translation of the trial record I used is by W. S. Scott. The text was taken from an original known as the Orléans Manuscript.

I am greatly indebted to the generosity of two of my colleagues at Barnard College: Joel Kaye of the Department of History and Christopher Baswell of the Department of English. I also wish to thank Joanne MacNamara, Professor Emerita of History at Hunter College.

For his heroic patience and help, my thanks go to my husband, Arthur Cash, frustrated military historian and footnote fetishist extraordinaire, whose distinction as a biographer humbles me as a would-be colleague, but fills me with pride as an actual wife.

Contents

Chronological Table

1337		The Hundred Years' War begins
1412	*Jan. 6 probably*	Birth of Joan of Arc
1420		The Treaty of Troyes
1424	*Midsummer probably*	Joan first hears the voices
1428	*July*	Flight to Neufchâtel
1429	*Jan.–Feb.*	Visit to Vaucouleurs
	Feb. 23	Joan leaves Vaucouleurs for Chinon
	March 6	Arrival at Chinon
	March 9 (approx.)	Received by the dauphin
	March–April	At Chinon, Poitiers, Tours, and Blois
	April 28	Arrival before Orléans
	April 29	Enters Orléans
	April 29–May 10	At Orléans
	May 7	Journée des Tourelles
	May 8	The siege raised
	May 10	Departure from Orléans
	June 11–12	Capture of Jargeau
	June 15	At Meung-sur-Loire
	June 16–17	Capture of Beauregency
	June 18	Battle of Patay
	July 17	Charles VII crowned
	July 21	Charles VII and Joan leave Rheims

1429	*Aug. 12*	At Lagby-le-Sec
	Aug. 18–23	At Compiègne
	Aug. 26–Sept. 8	At St.-Denis and La Chapelle
	Sept. 8	Attack on Paris (Joan wounded)
	Sept. 9	La Chapelle and St.-Denis
	Sept. 10 and 13	At St.-Denis
	Sept. 13	Departure from St.-Denis for the Loire
	Nov. 24	Attack on La Charité
1430	*April*	Battle of Lagny
	May 23	Compiègne and assault on Margny; Joan taken prisoner
	? May, June, July	At Beaulieu, a prisoner
	Dec. 25–May 30	Prisoner in a tower of castle of Phillipe Auguste, Rouen
1431	*Jan. 3*	Delivered to the Inquisition and the Church by the English
	Jan. 9	Trial begins
	May 24	The recantation
	May 30	Burned at the stake
1450		Examination of witnesses for the rehabilitation begins, under the direction of Guillaume Bouillé
1452		Resumes under Cardinal d'Estouteville, bishop of Digne, and Jean Brehal, inquisitor of France
1455–1456		Continued by order of Pope Calixtus III
1456	*July*	The sentence revoked by Pope Calixtus III

Introduction

She is one of the few figures in history who cannot be anything but protagonists, who are never subordinate, always an end and never a means.

—JOHAN HUIZINGA

Charisma ... bursts the bonds of rules and tradition and overturns all ideas of the sacred. It enforces a subjection to something which has never before existed.

—MAX WEBER

Youth forgets itself in its own ardor.... When youth has once grasped where beauty dwells, its self-surrender is absolute.

—ALFRED NORTH WHITEHEAD

MARCH 14, 1999. The city of Rouen, the province of Normandy, the country of France, the continent of Europe. It is 5 P.M. on an unseasonably warm spring day. People have flung their jackets over their shoulders. They are sitting outside in cafés, reckless from the sunlight, which seems miraculous, unearned, suggestive of improvidence.

We are in the marketplace, the place where Joan of Arc was burned at the stake. An attempt has been made to make this a viable city center; there is an open space for a market and, next to it, a cathedral. It is one of those good ideas that didn't work; it might have worked had there been a genius to design it, but it was not designed by a genius. The church is in the shape of an overturned boat, and the motif is meant to be nautical: Rouen is a seafaring city. But the idea fails; it provides us only with the always dispiriting spectacle of overstrained originality. The church has the sad, earnest quality of mediocre modern architecture, and we are left with a sense of betrayal, because we think that plain materials and an abundance of light ought to equal beauty, and when they don't, not only art, but nature as well, has let us down.

It is a Sunday, late afternoon. A ruddy light hangs low over the pavement. In the way of failed modern spaces, this one has become a haven for the underemployed, unprosperous young. Boys with greasy hair and tattoos throw their cigarette butts onto the ground. Two other, younger boys are throwing a soccer ball, with a disturbing violence, against the wall of the marketplace. They throw it against the words André Malraux wrote in 1964 when he dedicated this complex: *"Jean d'Arc, sans sepulchre et sans portrait, toi qui savais que le tombeau des heros est le coeur des vivants."* ("Joan of Arc, without tomb and without portrait, you who knew that the grave of heroes is the heart of the living.") I try to read the words between the blows of the soccer ball—*blam,*

blam, goes the leather against the concrete, leaving only narrow windows of legibility.

A little to the left of the wall is a public toilet out of which boys skulk. Suddenly, there is the sound of girls shouting. Everyone in the area stands still. The two girls, both wearing jeans and boots and sleeveless shirts, are punching each other. One throws the other to the ground and straddles her, hitting her face. A boy stands in the background, ineffectually urging them to stop. No one from the watching crowd moves to stop them. Then the police come, and everyone scatters. There is one small patch of blood on the concrete slope that leads from the church to the surrounding street.

In this spot, over five hundred years ago, a girl the same age as the two fighting girls gave up her life. This shocks us still, as we were shocked by the violence of the two fighting girls—far more than we would have been by fighting boys. Girls are not supposed to be violent. But girls are not supposed to be warriors, whose métier is, after all, violence. They are not supposed to be burned alive. It is precisely the disjunction between our expectations of what girls should do and the shape of Joan of Arc's life that has been, for half a millennium, a source of fascination.

She must be thought of as a girl. Our understanding of her must always be enclosed in the envelope of her age and gender. She was young and female, and the interpretation of her acts is inevitably colored at each moment by these two facts.

She referred to herself as "La Pucelle." The Maid. Included in her self-description, in the almost heraldic tag by which she wished herself to be known, is a statement about her sexual state: She is a young virgin. But one tinged by romance. So before we look at the facts, we have to pass through our associations with girlhood: desirability, charm, innocence, a kind of claustral protectedness suggested by Yeats's "Prayer for My Daughter."

> May she become a flourishing hidden tree
> That all her thoughts may like the linnet be . . .
> Nor but in merriment begin a chase,
> Nor but in merriment a quarrel.
> Oh may she live like some green laurel
> Rooted in one dear perpetual place.

But this girl was a soldier, and the word *soldier* forces us to put on a very different pair of spectacles from the one we use to watch a girl. Soldiers must be in the thick of things. They protect us; they are not protected. Innocence is a luxury they indulge in to our peril, and their own. God help us all, and them, if they only begin a chase or a quarrel in merriment or if they root themselves in one place alone.

Joan, the girl/soldier, forces us to bathe in two waters of vastly different qualities and temperatures, as if we were swimming simultaneously in a raging ocean and a warm, enclosed lake. The demand for an equilibrium that can tolerate such contradictory elements is a difficult one. Few have endured it. She doesn't make it easy for us, and most have settled for a Joan whose contradictions have been air-brushed away in favor of a single, static portrait that is primarily a mirror of their own desires.

There is no one like her.

There is no one like her.

We pretend to believe that about all human beings. We cannot know ourselves to be ourselves without believing that we would cry out—knife to our throats, gun to our heads—our convictions about the uniquenesses, the non-interchangeability, of each human life. But we don't live that way; we can't. We put our faith in correspondences. We test for DNA; we say, "What can you expect from that neighborhood," or, "Boys will be boys." We speak of Renaissance man, founding fathers.

But Joan stands on a bare plain, unresembled. She has neither forebears nor descendants. She may be the one person born before 1800, with the exception of Jesus Christ, that the average Westerner can name. The man on the street can even create an image of her: the girl in armor. He can say that she is French, that she died young. He knows she wore men's clothing. Try to name anyone else in history about whom the popular imagination calls up three facts. Nero? Napoleon? There are local gods—Lincoln, Garibaldi—but could a Spanish child, or a Danish one, identify their faces in a lineup? An Indian friend has told me that as a child, Indira Gandhi played at being Joan of Arc. What other historical character creates a force field so extensive and so wide?

Her rivals are the characters of myth. Robin Hood, King Arthur. But Joan lived in history, and most of what the popular mind knows about her can be verified in trial testimony. Unlike other historical figures, we need not invent stories to flesh her out (there is no chopped-down cherry tree). We need to create nothing; our need is, rather, to suppress.

For we need in her an image of singularity and single-mindedness. A girl, her foot shod in metal ending in a sharp point, digging its way forever into one piece of earth. In fact, she was erratic and self-contradictory, and her real fascination lies in the way that these contradictions did not end in the stillness and silence of her death.

The facts can be quickly related. She was born in Domrémy in the current province of Lorraine, in January 1412. Her land was devastated by the Hundred Years' War, a dynastic conflict with England that began in 1337.

Her father was a peasant with some local standing: He represented the town in the local assizes. She had three brothers. She was trained in the traditional female skills and sometimes tended sheep. Sometime around her twelfth birthday, she began hearing sacred voices that spoke to her first about the need for her to preserve her virginity for the salvation of her soul. Later, their message became more specific: She must crown the dauphin king and save France from the English.

She convinced the local lord to give her entrée to the king, whom she convinced to outfit her so that she could participate in lifting the siege of Orléans. Her presence at the siege turned the tide so that the French were, for the first time in a long time, victorious. She crowned the dauphin in the city of Rheims. But soon her military fortunes turned, and she engaged in a series of failed battles that ended in her capture by the Burgundians, whose duke, a relative of the French king, had allied himself with the English. She was sold to the English, tried by French ecclesiastics, and sentenced to death by burning.

The most important character in this story, aside, that is, from Joan herself, is faceless. This character is time. The element of time gives Joan's history a special poignance. First, it is the creator and the warden of her youth. She was seventeen when she left her village to head an army. This is rather well known. What is not well known is the brevity of her career, particularly its successful aspects. She was successful militarily for less than six months. She was an active soldier for a little more than a year. She was a prisoner longer than she was a warrior. She died at nineteen.

A brief career, and by ordinary standards an unsuccessful one. At the time of her death, her cause was losing. It would win, eventually, but only thirty years after her burning, and her role in the ultimate success of France is vexed; it has occupied scholars for pages and years. Why, then, do we remember her?

We do not call her up as a type of victim. We call her up as one who held back nothing—we don't examine too closely the justice of the cause. She came from nowhere and gave everything. She pitted herself against those who were far better endowed than she. She was illiterate, and female. She was always very, very young.

But would she have been considered young by her contemporaries? Doubts arise when we think even as far back as our own grandparents, who seemed to take on extraordinary responsibilities in the years when we were still in our dorm rooms, waking at noon from the overlong sleeps of adolescence. We think of Romeo and Juliet and royal marriages consummated at fifteen. Yet even for her time and place Joan, at seventeen, was extraordinary. If she had stayed at Domrémy and lived as a peasant, she might, by seventeen, have been a wife and mother and laboring fully in the life of the community. But she left the life of the peasant for the life of a knight, and a knight, at her age, having started his training more than ten years earlier, would at seventeen have only been beginning his career. He would not have been put at the head of anything. At eighteen, Lancelot was joining Arthur's men for the first time.[I]

There was a medieval term for adolescence, *adolescentia*, but its boundaries were unfixed. Dante put its end point at forty-five. Following Roman law, in many medieval societies young men under twenty-five were not allowed to carry out certain actions without a guardian and before this point were not permitted to exercise their full civil rights. Girls of the nobility were often married quite early, but this was because they had virtually no access to the arena of public action, where proper judgment would be crucial. Perhaps a better way of looking at Joan's youth is that in all her major battles she was younger than anyone she rode beside, and in all the important rooms of her life she was alone among her elders.

We would like to believe that youth, ardor, audacity, courage, and natural intelligence will prevail against bureaucratic power and corruption. In Joan's case, there is an important sense in which they did not. She died, after all, at her enemies' hands. But she stands for the triumph of the invisible over the visible, of the potency of pure intention, of acts that shimmer and endure beyond the life of the actor or the efficacy of the acts.

We have always needed someone like her, someone who can disinfect us of our disreputable or petty tendencies. If we can love her, then we are not a people who hate women. If we can call her death a triumph, we are not time servers, pension collectors who measure success only by what seems to work. If we devote ourselves to her, we are higher creatures than the way we live our lives suggests. We need her as the heroine of our better selves.

But she is much more interesting as herself than as the hero of our need of her. My Joan, who is just as much a mirror of my own desires as anyone else's, is, above all, a young girl. She has a young girl's heedlessness, sureness, readiness for utter self-surrender. She loves life; she is afraid of dying. This cocky, pure, maddening, unwise girl forgot herself in a cause greater than herself. She was talky and self-contradictory; she died in silence. But even in death she refuses singleness. So everyone who uses words to describe her must understand that her project is impossible, one or another kind of failure, one or another partial shot.

If I could, I would begin this study in a way that would defy the limits of space and time. I call it a study, or a meditation, hesitating over the honorable term *biography,* with its promise of authority, of scholarship, of scope and sweep. Ideally, I would present you not with pages, but with an envelope of paper strips, each with some words written on it, and a series of snapshots. I would have you open the envelope, drop the strips and photographs onto the floor, then pick them up and read them in whatever order they had arranged themselves in your hand. I would require, then, that you replace the strips in the envelope and empty them again. And pick them up again. And read and look again. And again, and again, giving pride of place to no one order. Until you had felt that you had understood something in a way that refused finality. That you could tolerate an understanding that allows that the fragments can be endlessly reordered, must be, and that the sense of knowing is always temporary, subject to revision, reversal, recombination, and a relaxation of the compulsion to know what is unknowable.

In writing what I think of as a biographical meditation,

I do homage to her instability. I involve myself in the task, unfinishable, of contemplating the mystery of a girl who came from nowhere, supported an equivocal cause, triumphed for a few months only, failed as a soldier, saw visions, abjured the primacy of her vision, then recanted her abjuration, died in agony, a saint whom the Church refused canonization for five hundred years, yet who stands in our imagination for the single-minded triumph of the she—and it must be a she—who feared nothing, knew herself right and fully able and the chosen of the Lord.

JOAN of ARC

CHAPTER I

OF HER TIME AND PLACE

THE FIRST DREAM of Joan of Arc was dreamed by her father. He saw his daughter traveling with an army: a camp follower.

When he awoke, he told her brothers that if this ever happened, he would ask them to drown her, and if they refused, he would do it himself. He communicated nothing of this to his daughter directly; her mother relayed it to her. Father fears for daughter's virtue and tells sons and mother: mother tells daughter. No surprises here.

It is profitless for us to look at Joan's family background for clues about her history. She was probably born on the Feast of the Epiphany, January 6, in the year 1412, the daughter of Jacques d'Arc, or Tart, and Isabelle, called Romée. Jacques d'Arc was a peasant in the village of Domrémy, on the border between the provinces of Champagne and Lorraine, distinguished only because he seems to have been a person of some local consequence; he was appointed the representative of the villagers in a suit that had been brought against Robert de Baudricourt, the lord of neighboring Vaucouleurs. Later, Baudricourt would give Joan her first official support.

Isabelle was given the name Romée because that was a sobriquet given to one who had participated in a long pilgrimage; this would indicate an unusual piety, and probably, as well, a somewhat unusual, though not unheard of, initiative in a young woman. Joan tells us that from her mother she learned her prayers, and the ordinary household tasks that would be taught to a young woman. With her characteristic boastfulness, she asserts that there was no one superior to her in sewing and spinning. She probably had charge of the sheep, although this was not so much a part of her daily life as iconography about her would indicate, and she probably drove the cattle from time to time, although she denied the importance of it at the trial, as if it suggested a lowness of occupation with which she was unwilling to associate herself. She had a sister and two brothers, the younger of whom accompanied her until her capture. After Joan's death, her brothers participated in a scheme to pass off an imposter as the real Joan, a kind of sideshow. They did it for the money.

But Joan's family does not seem to have been of much consequence to her. When she decided to obey her voices and go off to crown the king of France, she left home with a cousin, who was her godfather, employing an ordinary, adolescent lie. She told her parents she was going to help out with the cousin's wife's labor, and then with the new child. She never spoke to her parents again, and when she was asked during her trial if she felt guilty about what could only be construed as a sin of disobedience, she said, "Since God commanded it, had I had a hundred fathers and a hundred mothers, had I been born a king's daughter, I should have departed."[1]

So we would do well not to linger over Joan's family for explanations of anything. Like any genius, Joan resists attempts to trace the nature of her history in clues from antecedents. She is an impossibility, a puzzlement, and yet she did come from somewhere. It is probably more useful to look at the larger context of her early life than at the narrow sphere of the domestic, which she could hardly wait to leave.

The State

The Hundred Years' War is one of those historical events or epochs to which the imagination is not naturally drawn. The late fourteenth and early fifteenth centuries can be thought of as the otiose and yet malnourished rump of the Middle Ages. The major war was not a cataclysmic horror but the drawn-out dance of nearly a century of fruitless and debilitating destruction. Rather than imagining a great blaze, we should think of a series of small brushfires that are never put out but smolder continually, creating a noxious smoke and sparking other small fires in the vicinity, filling the air with poisonous vapors and destroying the land's possibilities for productive habitation. The population of France had been decimated by plagues and famine in the fourteenth century, but now the countryside was being devastated not as the result of great battles but because of the marauding of the armies when they were not en-

gaged. These freebooters, called *écorcheurs,* or fleecers, rav-
aged the land looking for spoils—the only way they could
support themselves, since the powers who had hired them
(England and France) could not raise enough money to
pay them properly. Ostensibly the war was fought under
the banner of chivalry, but the gap between the chivalric
ideal and the behavior of those who claimed it was enormous. The *écorcheurs* were not noble themselves, but their
behavior was tolerated by nobles who turned a blind eye.

The people of the countryside had to contend with a
shifting cast of ravagers, and all the divisions of this vexed
society were mirrored in the mixed origins of the *écorcheurs.*
The mix was made more complex by the fact that the
marauders whom we would think of as "French" were
composed of two separate and warring factions, the Armagnacs and the Burgundians. At the time of Joan's birth,
France was not only at war with England; it was also in a
state of virtual civil war, the rich duchy of Burgundy
having allied itself with the English against the French
monarchy.

The Burgundian marauders were the ones whose effect
Joan and her family most closely felt. In 1425 the Burgundians, and some English, drove off the cattle of the inhabitants of Domrémy, and the church was burned and
plundered; 1425 was the year that Joan first heard her
voices. The juxtaposition of Joan's first experience of civil
violence and the onset of her puberty may be one of those
historical accidents that suggest more than they finally
explain. But, no doubt, the witnessing of hatred and dis-

order at a vulnerable time in her life marked Joan permanently. In 1428, months before she left Domrémy on her mission to crown the dauphin, her family had to flee their home for the neighboring town of Neufchâtel as a result of Burgundian marauders. It was here that Joan worked at the inn of a woman called La Rousse, generating later rumors that she had consorted with soldiers. It was here, and no earlier, that she learned to ride a horse.

Joan was clear, when she spoke during her trial of her early years, that the Burgundians were her chief enemy and that Domrémy was united in its hatred of them. With her usual avoidance of understatement she said, "I knew of only one Burgundian there, and I could have wished his head cut off—however only if it pleased God."[2] But just across the river Meuse, in the neighboring town of Maxey, the citizens were supporters of Burgundy. The children of both villages would come home bloody from fighting over loyalties to the duke or the king. It is tempting to wonder what would have become of Joan had she been born on the other side of the river Meuse, where devotion was not to the beleaguered king but to the duke who had allied himself across the Channel.

This confusion of affiliations is an index of the disorder of the times and the muddled loyalties that a nature like Joan's, thriving on clarity, must have found as anguishing as the burning of her church and the destruction of her neighbors' cattle. But muddle and confusion are the hallmark of the Hundred Years' War, which victimized thousands because of an unclear dynastic claim, a problem created by the fact that the royal families of England and France were closely related by blood.

The dynastic muddle begins with Edward II of England. He claimed the French crown as a result of his being the grandson of Philip IV, the French king, who died in 1314. Philip's three sons had no male issue; Edward was the child of Philip's daughter, Isabella. When the youngest of Philip's sons died, the contenders to the throne were Edward of England and Count Philip of Valois. Philip of Valois was the son of the dead king Philip's younger brother. Edward's claim to the throne was, therefore, a generation nearer to the crown than Philip of Valois's, but its validity was weakened because it came through the female line. Whether this invocation of the "salic law" was in fact valid, or just a ploy used by the French to prevent having an Englishman on their throne, has been a matter for scholarly debate.

In 1337, Philip of Valois, after declaring Edward a "contumacious vassal," confiscated the duchy of Gascony, which the English considered theirs since the time of Eleanor of Aquitaine (1122–1204). Edward, unwilling to give up his sovereignty in Gascony, waged war with France. But the economic conditions at home made it a half-hearted effort for the English, and for some years the war went on with no clear victory on either side, only misery for the peasants who were its victims, particularly the victims of the underpaid, underemployed soldiers. Then in 1346, the English scored a decisive victory at the Battle of Crecy, and ten years later they did the same at the Battle of

Poitiers, during which time King John of France was captured by the English and held for ransom. He died in London in 1364. Under the leadership of his son Charles V, an intelligent and able ruler with little stomach for war, France prospered while England was too absorbed in its own domestic troubles to continue the fight. Charles V's reign lasted from 1364 to 1380; he was succeeded by his son Charles VI.

Enter Henry V, the first English king strong enough to devote himself to full-scale operations in France. Henry was both a great king and a great general. His counterpart in France, Charles VI, was probably a paranoid schizophrenic subject to long bouts of insanity. The Battle of Agincourt, in 1415, won the French crown for Henry's heir, and he persuaded the defeated Charles VI to give him his daughter Catherine in marriage, thus strengthening his claim to the French crown. But both Henry V and Charles VI died in the same year, 1422. Henry's one-year-old son, Henry VI, and Charles VII, then nineteen, were both proclaimed kings of France.

Echoes of this dynastic struggle are familiar to us from Shakespeare: Richard II's errors of extravagance are set against the backdrop of the economic disaster of the Hundred Years' War; and the breach that Henry V rode into was at Agincourt—his victory there resulting in untold hardship for the French population. Even though Henry's soldiers were, as a result of his good leadership, relatively better disciplined than their predecessors (Pistol, Henry's former friend, is executed for brigandage), the French still had endured seventy years of devastation, during which English troops plundered their stores of food and wine, stole their harvests, drove their cattle from their fields, feasted in their towns by night and set them aflame in the morning. The noble soldiers with the golden tongues whom we encounter in Shakespeare were of the same party as the brutish mercenaries whom the French, including Joan, knew by their constant curse "goddamns" (rendered by them as "godons," their name for their invaders).

And lest we forget what the real implications of the dynastic claims were, we should try to imagine an English France. An extension of the island kingdom across the channel: a Normandy, Brittany, Provence, all English-speaking, a cultural history in which there was only cheddar and no brie, only Congreve and no Molière, only Chippendale and no French Provincial, only Turner and no Monet. In our time we have seen the ravages of nationalism so clearly that it is easy to think of it only as a curse, but to imagine the flattening out of culture that could have occurred if the English had won the Hundred Years' War is a deeply dispiriting mental exercise.

Joan, then, came into a world tainted with political and economic disorder, and the moral tone of the society reflected this. Abuses were rampant; the countryside starved while the king's court was luxurious. The atmosphere of the time was a dark cloud of depression and entropy. It is against this gray-brown background that the girl in white armor, on her black horse, placed herself.

The Church

If the state was in disarray, the Church was no better. At the time of Joan's birth in 1412, there were three claimants to the papacy: one in Rome, one in Avignon, and one in Spain. She was born into a Church torn by schism, and at the time of her death, although a council of the world's bishops had removed all the contenders to the papal throne from office and elected a new one, Martin V, the old Spanish pope, Benedict XIII, despite the fact that he had no authority and no followers, would still not give up his claim.

The history of the Great Schism is an indication of the mutually infecting relationship between a civil and religious order. Originally, the first Avignon pope had moved there because internal wars in Italy made it impossible for an orderly running of the Church's affairs to take place in Rome. But Avignon was in France, and France was involved in a war with England; England and her allies—particularly Germany and Italy—naturally resented the profits that would accrue to France as a result of the papacy's being centered there, so they put pressure on the Church to return the seat of St. Peter to Rome. In 1378, when the cardinals met in Rome to elect a pope, the population of Rome stormed the streets, demanding the election of an Italian. Probably in response to this, the cardinals elected

Bartholomew, archbishop of Bari. Urban VI, as he was known, was a man of such violence of temper that all the cardinals fled his vicinity in Rome and moved back to Avignon to elect another pope, claiming that the election was invalid, since it had been motivated by fear of the crowd. The cardinals elected a Frenchman who took the name of Clement VII.

But Urban would not withdraw his papacy, so there were two popes, both with legitimate claims to having been properly elected. Neither Clement nor Urban possessed admirable qualities. Abuses and corruption were particularly egregious, largely motivated by the Church's constant need for new sources of money as a result of newly powerful monarchs unwilling to knuckle under to papal demands for revenue. Urban was interested in speaking to these abuses, but his approach was to insult and bully his enemies; Clement seems to have had no impulse to attend to corrupt practices at all.

This corruption led to the rise of such reformers as John Wycliffe in England, and his disciple in Bohemia, Jan Hus. Wycliffe and Hus were appalled by the greed of the clergy and the hierarchy, and their distance from the people whom they were meant to serve. They advocated the use of reason in coming to spiritual and moral conclusions, and a translation of the Bible into the vernacular in order that it could be more widely available to the people.

Wycliffe's teachings had comparatively little immediate effect in England, but Hus had an enormous following in the kingdom of Bohemia, where the university's popular anticlericalism gave him an important base. His own popularity contributed to the Church's decision to burn him as a heretic in 1416.

It is easy to see the roots of Protestantism in the ideas of Wycliffe and Hus, and it is not difficult to understand the Church's unease at the power of this new, popular movement. Part of their anxiety about Joan can be traced to the threat they felt from popular movements which stressed private inspiration and the primacy of the individual conscience; in burning Joan, they believed they were burning a heretic; her death, mirroring Hus's, was a blow for orthodoxy against the disease of antiauthoritarian populism.

This spirit had expressed itself in the secular realm by revolts among the lower orders—the jacquerie in Champagne, Picardy, and Beauvais, and the artisans of London—all these taking place in the last years of the fourteenth century. Every word out of Joan's mouth at her trial reinforced the clerics' suspicions; they could hardly have invented speech that could more clearly have indicated her insistence on the primacy of her own vision over the authority of the Church.

This authority had been remarkably shored up after the disaster of the schism by the success of the Council of Constance and the election of Pope Martin V in 1417. When Joan came on the scene in 1429, the Church was determined to hold on to the authority it had been successfully wielding for a dozen years. Its new sense of authority expressed itself in an increased appetite for enforcing orthodoxy—as seen in the execution of Jan Hus.

The newly shored-up Church understood the sources and limits of its power. It had to contend with a world of powerful monarchs—it could not afford to ignore the wishes of kings as it had a century earlier. This new understanding of itself as a player in a geopolitical game made the Church much more aware of the need to ally itself with the strong rather than the weak. With France in a state of chaos, the choice to connect itself with England and its allies rather than France was a clear one for the Roman Church. This would have tragic consequences for Joan.

While these struggles for power were playing themselves out in the larger arena, on a local level, the late-fourteenth- and early-fifteenth-century Church was replete with lively popular activity, which took its form in an active folk tradition, visionary activity of a private, mystical nature, and apocalyptic preaching whose fiery tone roused the populace to ardor. St. Bernardino of Siena and St. Vincent Ferrer were both charismatic, colloquial speakers whose bonfire-of-the-vanities rhetoric attracted huge followings.

The grafting of pre-Christian and popular customs onto Christian practice was a cause of great anxiety to a Church which was all too aware of rumblings of rebellion and discontent. This was reflected in the behavior of Joan's judges during her trial. They seemed almost fixated on the popular folk practices of the villagers of Domrémy. They concentrated on a local custom of dancing around what was called the fairy tree. Joan seemed bored by their interest in fairies; she asserted that she never saw one, that some people in the town said there were some, but she had no knowledge of that. She spoke about some of her play with the other girls, and we get a picture of what is unusual in Joan's history: an ordinary life. She said that she hung garlands on the fairy tree and that she danced there with the other children, but that she "sang more often than she danced." It is a charming moment in the trial: Joan's care to distinguish between the childish activities of singing and dancing, giving pride of place to singing as if to make sure that at least in this happy occupation she was clearly and properly seen.

Joan answered all her judges' questions about superstitious or cult practices impatiently, speaking offhandedly about her ring, its powers, and the veneration of the public. She said her ring was a present from her parents. She admitted that she did cure a baby who was presented to her "as black as my cloak," but she had no interest in claiming that it was her own power that effected the cure, and she reiterated that she discouraged being made a cult figure. Religious life was always connected to action with her; the aspects of it that were merely pious had no place in her imagination.

Certain popular legends, however, served Joan very well in that they made a place in the public mind for someone like her. Many prophecies, from widely diverse sources, were abroad in Joan's time about a maiden who would save

France. The earliest is from the Arthurian wizard Merlin, who prophesied that a marvelous maid would come from the *Bois Chesnu*, the ancient wood, to save France. A response to the scandalous behavior of Isabeau of Bavaria, mother of Joan's dauphin, was the prophecy that a virgin would save France after a fallen woman had shamed it. Marie d'Avignon, a woman with a reputation as a prophet, had, some years earlier, foretold the arrival of someone like Joan at the dauphin's court. "She spoke of having had frequent visions concerning the desolation of France. In one of them Marie saw pieces of armor that were brought before her, which frightened her. For she was afraid that she would be forced to put this armor on. But she was told to fear nothing, that it was not she who would have to wear this armor, but a Maid who would come after her who would wear it and deliver the kingdom of France from its enemies."[3]

Joan's history becomes somewhat less baffling when one remembers the importance of the prophetic and the mystical in the mind of her time. Whether or not she understood that the *Zeitgeist* was making a place for her, she took the place brilliantly. And some of the most important people who made Joan's way possible were the female mystics of the generations immediately preceding her. Notable among them were Bridget of Sweden (d. 1373) and Catherine of Siena (d. 1380), whose activities in relation to the Great Schism earned her the rank of doctor of the

Church. Closer to Joan's home, and her nearer contemporary, was St. Colette of Corbie. She was born in northern France in 1381 and devoted herself to reform of the order of the Poor Clares. There were rumors that she and Joan encountered each other and that she gave Joan the ring inscribed with the words "Jesus Maria," emblem of the popular cult of the Holy Names. In fact, the women never met.

The assumption of the mantle of prophecy was one of the few ways by which medieval women could speak with public authority, certain of being listened to. Because Joan invoked the words of her supernatural visitors as the authority for her mission, she shares in this tradition. But though Joan was extremely pious and had experienced visions involving angels and saints, both the quality of her visions and the shape of her life mark her as radically different from the mystics who preceded her. The language and imagery of the great mystics is hypersensualized, and hyperspecific in its accumulation of physical detail. It is, however, often short on facts about the realm of action in this world. Joan's descriptions of her visions were cut-and-dried, matter-of-fact. She spoke of "a great light" and a "great Pleasure." She was—to her later peril when her prophecies were not fulfilled—extremely specific about the plans her voices had for her. During her trial she had to be forced to be concrete about the appearance of St. Michael, St. Catherine, and St. Margaret, the angels and the saints who appeared to her and told her what she was to do. Contrast this lack of emphasis on physical detail with the acute focus of, say, the English medieval mystic Margery Kempe, a near contemporary of Joan's, who eroticizes and radically physicalizes her encounter with God.

> Thus she had a very contemplation in the sight of her soul as if Christ had hung before her bodily eye in his manhood. And . . . it was granted to this creature to behold so verily his precious tender body, all rent and torn with scourges, fuller of wounds than ever was a dovecote full of holes, hanging on the cross with the crown of thorns upon his head, his beautiful hands, his tender feet nailed to the hard tree, the rivers of blood flowing out plenteously from every member.[4]

This is a different imagistic and linguistic universe from Joan's straightforward answer to the judges' questions about St. Michael: "He was in the form of a true and honest man, and as for the clothes and other things, I shall not tell you any more."[5] When asked if he was naked, she replied impatiently, "Do you think that God cannot afford to clothe him," and when questioned as to whether he had hair, she snapped, "Why should it have been cut off?"[6]

Joan's history with an apocalyptic preacher, Brother Richard, reveals her uneasy relationship with the mystical. Richard's themes were the approach of the millennial Antichrist, the vanity of riches, and the perfidy of the Jews. In 1429 he fled Paris, prophesying the coming of great things. On the alert for marvels, his eye was caught by Joan, and he was sent by the people of Troyes to approach her and judge her fitness for their loyalty. At her trial, she gave a brusque version of their first meeting. "When he came to me, as he approached me, he made the sign of the cross, and sprinkled Holy water, and I said to him: 'Approach boldly—I shall not fly away.'"[7]

Despite her later flippant account, Joan was taken for a time with Richard, as he shared her devotion to the cult of the Holy Name and encouraged her in her predilection for taking Communion frequently—sometimes as often as three times a day, which would have been heterodox at the time. But they fell out because he attached himself to another female prophet, who irritated Joan in the way that only a female rival can irritate another female. Joan knew herself to be the real thing, and she quickly spotted Catherine de la Rochelle as a fake. Catherine was supposed to have had visions of a white lady who came to her at night. Joan challenged her: She would spend the night beside her, and if the white lady came, she would see her as well. When the white lady never showed up, Joan told Catherine to go back to her husband and her children. We can hear in these words the echo of the professional woman's contempt for the part-timer. After Joan's huffy dismissal of Catherine, her relationship with Brother Richard never recovered.

Although it is easy to distinguish Joan from other mystics or pseudomystics, we should not go too far in this direction and forget that she was, at her core, a person moved by a religious vision. Like everything else about her, the nature of her religious life was mixed; there was a strong sprinkling of the practical and the political about it. There is no doubt, however, that she would have been incapable of doing the sometimes literally incredible things she did if she were not convinced to the depths of her soul that she was inspired by God. She often separated herself from the soldiers for private prayer, from which she would return refreshed and visibly illuminated. She spoke of the delight of the presence of her voices. She insisted that the men under her rise to an acceptable level of morality and piety, and worried that her enemies might die unshriven. She was never without God except in the few moments before and after her abjuration when she saw herself, like Christ in the Garden, abandoned. But for most of her life, she understood herself to be constantly and palpably in the company of the divine. It is this source of companionship that provided her remarkable sureness, her superhuman courage, her faith in her own authority.

Joan's formal religious training was rudimentary; she tells us that she learned her Pater Noster from her mother, and she spoke of no other religious instruction, from the local priest or any other church authority. Her speech is remarkably free of biblical allusion; illiterate, she would have learned what she knew of the Scripture from what she heard at mass. She also made no mention of devotion to the Virgin Mary, although Marian cults were popular during the period in which she lived. She related to Christ as "her lord" but offered no details of personal intimacy and did not focus on His Passion, although Franciscan and Dominican spirituality, with which she would have been

familiar, as her mother had gone on pilgrimages with mendicant friars and her confessor was a Dominican, stressed
gory physical details of Christ's Passion and death. In her
moments of suffering, she did not link herself with the
suffering of Jesus. She was loyal to God, as she was loyal to
the king: she would be loyal to the Church except that the
Church represented by her accusers she defined not as the
Church (the Church was the pope in Rome) but as her enemies. Above all, she was loyal to her voices, whose divine
source she never doubted.

As historical character, model, or exemplum, Joan would
be far more palatable to the post-Enlightenment appetite if
she hadn't claimed to hear voices. As it is, her definition of
herself is impossible without them, and it is expected, presumably, of any writer about Joan to take a position about
them. A comfortable position for our time might be a contemporary version of De Quincey's, who tried to paint
Joan's experience in Kate Greenaway colors. "On a fine
breezy forenoon, I am audaciously skeptical, but as twilight
sets in, my credulity grows steadily, till it becomes equal to
anything that could be desired. . . . Fairies are important,
even as in a statistical view certain weeds mark poverty in
the soil, fairies mark its solitude."[8]

Thomas De Quincey was a great lover of Joan, and he
was trying to brush away the problems that nineteenth-
century Protestants—including, probably, himself—might
have with her. In the same way, George Bernard Shaw's assertion that her voices were her own "common sense"

makes her acceptable to a skeptical, rational freethinker. But we do her an injustice to think of her experience without honoring the terms in which she thought of it: as a religious one. Joan's voices urged her to do things that common sense would find impossible and that a "fairies-in-the-garden" sensibility would find appalling. They urged her to leave home, to become a soldier, to engage in war, to risk her life and lead men into battle to crown a king. She did this not for personal gain, which never occurred to her, or for fame, which also never entered her mind, but because she believed herself to be called and because not to do so would seem to her a betrayal of everything sacred and precious.

The voices are dear to her: She speaks of her joy in their presence, her sense of bereftness when they leave her. Although her language is far less florid than that of the female mystics, she uses the synesthetic image of light—a combination of sound and vision—that is a commonplace in descriptions of the mystical experience. The experience of her voices happens to her on the deepest level of a creature of flesh, blood, mind, and spirit; the whole of herself is absorbed in the vision that emanates from what she knows to be the source of love and truth and salvation. De Quincey's and Shaw's responses to her voices recall Mary McCarthy's attempt to make Flannery O'Connor's literal belief in the Eucharist acceptable. Helpfully, McCarthy suggested that the presence of Christ in the Eucharist was symbolic. Flannery O'Connor retorted, "If I thought it was symbolic, I'd say the hell with it."

Far more apt, I believe, is the analysis of Johan Huizinga, whose beautiful and elegant work on the medieval period grants him an unquestionable scholarly authority about the mind of the age. He explains in his essay "Bernard Shaw's Saint" that the reason he didn't include Joan of Arc in his milestone work *The Waning of the Middle Ages* was that he was afraid her vivid presence would overwhelm and overbalance the book. He suggests that Joan's expressing her experience as divinely sent voices was uncommon but not bizarre for the time, that to the contemporary framework of understanding it was no more odd than a twentieth-century person speaking of her unconscious or of outer space or relativity. He vehemently denies that her voices are pathological, and his work has not hesitated in pointing to the pathology of the age in which she lived. Her experience was unusual, he says, but it was not disturbed.

> We know that an anomaly only becomes a sickness when it has a disturbing effect on the purpose of the organism. And Joan's voices may have had a very disturbing influence on her lower purpose of enjoying life and growing old, but it is not on such things that we would like to base our conclusion.

One can hear the impatience in his usually quiet measured voice when he answers the charge of mental imbalance as the source of Joan's voices:

> If every inspiration that comes to me with such commanding urgency that it is heard as a voice is to be con-

demned out of hand by a learned qualification of a morbid symptom, a hallucination, who would not rather stand with Joan of Arc and Socrates than with the faculty of the Sorbonne on that of the sane.[9]

Huizinga's defense of Joan's voices is different from that of the Catholic apologists before and after Joan's canonization, who used Joan's voices as a proof of the justice of the Catholic cause—and the French one. Huizinga was a Dutch Moravian with no particular brief for either Catholicism or French nationalism.

It is interesting to examine how Joan's descriptions of her voices changed during the course of the trial. As the trial went on, pressed by her judges, she became more and more specific about the identity of the voices and their physical appearance. The historian Karen Sullivan believes that this greater specificity was, in fact, a product of the language of the questions that the judges asked, an absorption, as a result of her desperation and exhaustion, of her accusers' terms and a rejection of her own nonclerical, vernacular ones.

Sullivan notes that the judges were clerics formed by scholastic philosophy, the system of thought of St. Thomas Aquinas, famous for its method of finding truth through relentless dividing and questioning. His discussion of angels includes their movements, their knowledge, their hierarchy, whether they move through intermediate space, whether they know singular facts or only universal ones. She says that the chronicles describing Joan written by laypeople who knew Joan when she was alive don't refer to her voices as being embodied in the persons of St. Michael, St. Catherine, and St. Margaret, but merely speak of them as the voice of "God." In tracing the trial testimony, she finds that Joan refused to specify the nature of her voices for the first three days of the trial. It was only when she was asked "if it was the voice of an angel that spoke to her, or if it was the voice of a saint or God without intermediary, that she responded that it was the voice of St. Catherine and St. Margaret and their faces are crowned with beautiful crowns, very opulent and precious." Even then, when asked about St. Michael's giving her comfort, she said, "I do not name to you the voice of St. Michael but I speak of a great comfort."[10]

A charitable interpretation of the judges' insistence on Joan's greater specificity is that it would be more in keeping with mystical tradition and would therefore give them a way of understanding it. A vague "it came from God" left them at sea, sailing uncharted waters. Joan confounded their attempts, however, by answering about her voices inconsistently. Sometimes she refused to answer the judges' questions; sometimes she answered their questions about the voices' identity by referring to her emotional response to the voices. In their summary of Joan's answers to their questions, however, the judges only focused on the answers that were in the terms they wanted: specific mentions of Michael, Catherine, and Margaret. As the trial progressed—it is possible to say, as Joan got more worn down—she spoke increasingly of the archangel Michael and the saints, and by the eleventh day, she had abandoned her vague terms from the beginning of the trial entirely.

Sullivan notes, however, that even if we understand that Joan's providing the judges with names was a result of the unrelenting pressure of their questions, the choice of the identities was hers. The culture of the veneration of saints was flourishing to the point of excess in Joan's time; the authorities of the Church were attempting to curb the endless proliferation of local saints, but their attempts were only beginning to be successful. This is to say that Joan had an enormous cast of characters to choose from if she were attaching specific names and faces to a voice that she initially experienced as an unspecified divine messenger.

Joan's choice of St. Michael, St. Catherine, and St. Margaret could be described as another example of her genius for self-presentation and the creation of highly legible signs. On the other hand, the choices can be read as a natural response typical of any pious girl from the Middle Ages to the present. For the faithful who venerate them, the saints provide both models and protection, and they are invoked for specific reasons connected to the narratives of their lives. Thus, even in our day, believers pray to St. Anthony to help them find lost things, to St. Jude for impossible causes, to St. Lucy, whose eyes were gouged out, for diseases of the eye. In my school, we were told to pray to St. Joseph Cupertino when studying for our exams on the ground that he was a poor student who prayed to be asked only the questions he had studied. This miracle was granted, and he was able to become a priest.

Female saints have an especially important function for young girls, since they provide examples of heroism outside the sphere of the domestic; the simplest girl has access to models who defied authority and made a place for themselves in the larger world. Joan herself has served this function for centuries of pious girls; she made sacred the longings for self-expression in the public world that in all other contexts would have been vilified.

The three saints that Joan invoked are vivid examples of the active, rather than the contemplative, path to sanctity. St. Catherine was the patron saint of philosophers and students; it makes sense that Joan would invoke her when she was up against the learned clerics.

Catherine died in 305. When the Roman emperor Maxentius ordered the execution of Christians, Catherine offered a learned discussion of the faith when she was brought before him. This inflamed him with desire, and he ordered her to marry him. When she refused him on the grounds of preserving her virginity as a bride of Christ only, he devised a machine with wheels to crush her, but the machine was miraculously disabled, leaving the frustrated executioners no choice but to behead her. Marina Warner says that Catherine "stood chiefly for independent thinking, courage, autonomy. She was the saint chosen by young unmarried women in France."[11]

One clear link between Joan and St. Margaret was that Margaret was one of those female saints who entered a monastery in the disguise of a man. Like Catherine, she was also martyred for refusing to marry a pagan, and she, too, was decapitated. Margaret was usually pictured with a sword, as was St. Catherine. All three of Joan's saints were armed, especially Michael, the protective angel of France. Mont-St.-Michel, in Normandy, was the last bastion of French loyalty. Michael was always represented in armor. So the three saints (one doubling as an angel) with whom Joan identified her voices were icons of resistance and might.

Everyone who spoke of Joan mentioned her great religious fervor. And yet she set herself up as superior to the authority of the Church, which gave her access to everything she loved, the Church which was the mystical body of the Christ whom she believed she served. She was devoted to the Eucharist but refused to give up men's clothing in order to receive it.

This does not, however, mark her as irreligious or as a crypto-Protestant. She challenged the followers of the rebel Jan Hus in Bohemia and threatened them with a crusade under her leadership—an example of her almost limitless sense of mission.

> I, Joan the Maid, to tell you true, I would have visited you long ago with my avenging arm if the war with the English had not kept me here. But if I do not hear soon that you have mended your ways, that you have returned to the bosom of the Church, I shall perhaps leave the English and turn against you, to extirpate the dreadful superstition with my blade of iron and to snatch you from heresy or from life itself.[12]

How, then, do we understand Joan's religious life? She was untutored theologically, yet was able to contend with the learning of the leaders of the University of Paris, to resist their charge of witchcraft and to maintain the integrity of her position on her voices. She was a loving daughter of the Church whose greatest moments of joy came from its prayer and its sacraments, yet she refused to allow herself this consolation if it meant denying what she knew to be her mission.

It is no easier to understand Joan as a religious figure than as a political or military one. She bursts out of categories, crisscrosses our ideas about her, contradicts the images she has presented about herself. We must make an attempt to place her historically, geographically, sociologically. Doing so may help us understand why what happened was not impossible, but does not explain the extremely unlikely fact that it happened at all. The life of Joan is such a flagrant beating of the odds that no facts sufficiently explain the course of it. She was born during one of the most corrupt, demoralized periods of French history; she is considered a religious and military hero, but she had neither religious nor military training. Her family was undistinguished; it was, if anything, an obstacle she had to overcome. She existed in time and space; she was a product of history and culture and was formed by them. But the Joan who transcended all the norms of where and when she was born must, if we honor her properly, remain, in her essential shape, mysterious.

CHAPTER II

APPROACHING THE THRONE

Joan's King

THE MESSENGERS who came to tell Joan the Word of God were heavenly creatures, but their message was specific and definitely of this world. She was charged by St. Catherine, St. Margaret, and St. Michael with the task of crowning the dauphin king of France. It was the French crown that shimmered always in front of her eyes, and her vision of the head that would wear it may have been blurred by the gold's ancient luster.

The man whom Joan would crown king of France was hardly the proper stuff of a young girl's dreams. As a man, he wasn't worth a hair on Joan's cropped head; as a leader, he was weak, equivocal, and self-serving. Yet it was the idea of crowning Charles that inspired Joan to leave her village and to give her life. This devout girl was moved not by a religious goal, not the simple salvation of her soul, the spreading of the Gospel, the conversion of the heathen Turks, or the recovery of the Holy Land. She didn't want to enter a convent or fast in a desert cave. She didn't want to inspire the unbelieving or the faint of heart. She wanted to crown a king, and the personality of the man whom she wanted to crown was of little importance to her.

Why would a girl who had never traveled more than ten miles from her home, who had never in her lifetime lived in a united France or under an honored monarch, be so fixed on the idea of endowing a wobbling dauphin with authority?

Part of the answer is that the idea of the sacredness of French kingship was probably the stuff of local lore. The image of a divinely bestowed kingship, made manifest by the symbol of the crown, was something that permeated French society. The legend of the sacred oil, carried in the beak of a dove in order to anoint Clovis, first king of the Franks, was readily available to Joan's imagination. Her parish church of Domrémy was dedicated to St. Remy, the patron saint of Rheims, the very place where the sacred oil was housed and the kings of France were anointed. There were local cults devoted to the sacred kingship of Clovis and Louis IX, and prayers were regularly offered to them for the protection of the king, who was seen to be under God's special care. That Joan would have been susceptible to such a religious iconography is evident by her naming St. Michael as one of the three saints who spoke to her in her visions. St. Michael was Charles VII's particular patron, and Charles had sponsored festivals and places of worship to encourage the association of himself with the Warrior Angel.

The symbols connected with the king: the crown and

the holy oil, the archangel Michael, and the kingship they represented may have served someone like Joan, who wanted order and clarity and singularity, with an image capable of creating a coherence that would be an alternative to the chaos and disorder that had constituted public life since her birth. But though it was a problem to create the image of a united France—particularly considering the civil war with Burgundy—the image of a single, divinely protected personage was much easier to come by. Certainly a French king would seem a solution to the horror wreaked by his enemies the Burgundians.

Perhaps Joan extended the idea that the enemy of my enemy is my friend to include the notion that the opponent of my marauder may be my salvation. In any case, after 1428, when the Burgundians invaded Domrémy, Joan's visions changed from the personal to the political; the saints spoke less of her preserving her virginity and more of her saving France. By the winter of 1428, or half a year after the Burgundians destroyed her home, Joan was fixed on the idea of making herself the soldier who would crown the king.

Joan may have imagined that Charles and his court were models of stability and order, but this was not the case. In fact, the entire history of Joan's imagination of Charles, and her relations with him, can be read as the conflict between mythical ideal and reality. The court of Charles VII was financially bankrupt, psychologically debilitated, and politically paralyzed. The butcher of Bourges refused to provide meat for the court on the grounds that he had not been paid, and for the same reason a cobbler refused to deliver slippers that Charles had ordered. Despite the financial realities, Charles felt compelled to keep up the extravagant and overelaborate court life that was a feature of the times, creating an atmosphere of decadent luxury and plunging himself further into debt. Margaret La Touroulde, wife of the king's receiver general, later one of Joan's hostesses, paints a dark picture of the state of Charles's court.

> When Joan came to the king at Chinon, I was at Bourges where the queen was. At that time there was in his kingdom and in those parts in obedience to the king such calamity and lack of money that it was piteous, and indeed those true to their allegiance to the king were in despair. I know it because my husband was at that time Receiver General and, of both the king's money and his own, he had not four crowns. And the city of Orléans was besieged by the English and there was no means of going to its aid. And it was in the midst of this calamity that Joan came, and I believe it firmly, she came from God and was sent to raise up the king and the people still within his allegiance for at that time there was no help but God.[1]

All of Charles's life, beginning with his birth, was lived under a star of disorder and ill governance. He was born in 1403, the eleventh child of his parents. At the time of his birth, two older brothers stood before him in the line of succession. His father was Charles VI of France, and his mother, the German princess Isabeau of Bavaria.

By the time Charles was born, his father had for years been subject to recurrent fits of madness, what in modern terms might be diagnosed as schizophrenia. He had his first attack in 1392, when he lost his mind during a military expedition and killed four attendants. He was sometimes violent and sometimes buffoonish; he suffered from hallucinations, such as believing that he was made of glass and had to carry pieces of iron in his clothing to protect himself. He refused to eat and sleep at regular hours; he allowed himself to become filthy and had to have his linen changed by force. Sometimes he would tremble and cry out that his body was being pricked by a thousand steel points.

In 1392, Charles became so insane that he couldn't rule at all; his brother Philip the Bold, duke of Burgundy, was made regent. Philip had married the heiress of Flanders and acquired her land, so he had aggregated an enormous amount of territory; this, in addition to his role as regent, made him immensely powerful. But when Charles was sane, he followed the advice, not of Philip, but of his other brother, Louis of Orléans. Both Burgundy and Orléans used their periods of power for their own ends; for example, each, when he was in favor, exempted his own lands from taxation. As a result of the king's mental illness, the French court was in a state of utter disarray.

Charles's mother, Isabeau, provided no countervailing force of stability. She was terrified of thunder and had a special conveyance built to protect her from it; she was phobic about disease and agoraphobic. She was frightened of crossing bridges and would cross none without a bal-ustrade. At the end of her life, she was grotesquely fat, to the point that her obesity made it doubtful that she could act as regent of the kingdom. She suffered from gout, and by 1425 she had to get around in a wheelchair. Pilgrimages were made in her name for her menstrual troubles.

Despite her weight, her shortness of leg and stature, and her ill health, she was infamous for her promiscuity. She was probably the lover of Louis of Orléans, her hus-band's younger brother. Her flagrant infidelities gave cre-dence to the belief that her son Charles was illegitimate. In the Treaty of Troyes, which she signed in 1420, she sug-gested that he was not the lawful heir to the French throne.

It is impossible to overestimate the importance of the uncertainty about Charles's legitimacy, both to him and to the state. The sacred power of the king was his, literally, by blood, and if the blood could not be traced to his father, he was on the throne, not by the will of God, but by a sub-terfuge. Questions of authority are always interpretive, and Charles's uncertain antecedents shook even the grounds upon which such an interpretation could be made.

In signing the Treaty of Troyes Isabeau agreed to an arrangement that disinherited her son and made Henry V of England heir to the French throne on the grounds that he had married Isabeau's daughter, Charles's sister Cather-ine. But the problems between Isabeau and Charles began with the death of Louis of Orléans. The rivalry between Louis, who was ruthless and brilliant, and his nephew John the Fearless, duke of Burgundy, had been a feature of Charles's life since his childhood. Louis had, in his own financial interest, cut off the flow of money from the French court to the dukedom of Burgundy. To pay him back, John had Louis murdered in 1407, and power vacillated between the Burgundians, led by John, and the Armagnacs, led by Bernard VII, count of Armagnac.

As a result of his marriage, Charles was in the camp of the anti-Burgundians. When he was fourteen but already married, Charles's last older brother died, and he became dauphin. Almost immediately, he quarreled with his mother, who sided with the Burgundians and lived under the protection of the duke of Burgundy (the murderer of her lover) at a dissolute but luxurious court. The duke's enemy, the count of Armagnac, who had possession of Paris and the loyalty of the dauphin, had Isabeau arrested and stripped of her wealth. She blamed her son for this.

In September 1419, Charles involved himself in the murder of John the Fearless, an act of vengeance for the assassination of Louis of Orléans. Although the actual murderer of John was never named, it was known that Charles was present on the bridge where an ax was buried in John's skull. For some reason, probably to safeguard her wealth and her place in the Burgundian court, Isabeau took sides against her son and in favor of the murderer of her former lover. The complications of Isabeau's relationship with Charles, her disloyalty to her son and the kingdom of France, are perplexing to the point of incomprehensibility.

Certainly the Treaty of Troyes is a historical anomaly: a mother explicitly supporting her son's enemies and implicitly casting doubts not only on his legitimacy but on her own sexual probity.

Charles inherited his mother's shortness of leg and was knock-kneed as well. His face was unprepossessing; his eyes were small and squinty, and his chin was weak. Although contemporary chroniclers praised his love of learning, everyone agreed that he was changeable and fickle in his loyalties. He had a habit of attaching himself to stronger, older men, most notably the duke de la Trémoille, who would never be a friend of Joan's.

De la Trémoille was a fat man of enormous height; he had the deepest pockets in France. His ready cash was responsible for his enormous influence, but probably his dominating physical presence had a humbling effect on weak, puny Charles. His policy was always one of diplomatic negotiation with the Burgundians rather than military confrontation with them and their British allies. In this, he was utterly opposed to Joan, who despised truces and felt that the Burgundians could only be spoken to "at the end of a lance."

De la Trémoille was famous as much for his girth as for his wealth; he was kept alive when an assassin's sword couldn't pierce his flesh. Iconically, this obese, wealthy, well-born courtier was exactly the opposite of the fleet, abstemious girl who came from nowhere, itching for a fight.

C'est le Premier Pas Qui Coute

The first step in Joan's remarkable journey is the most inexplicable, for it was the one she took unaccompanied by any sign of authority of gender or of class. She approached Robert de Baudricourt, the lord of her local bailiwick, escorted only by her godfather. She was seventeen years old and an illiterate peasant. She was asking for an army.

Myth has created Robert de Baudricourt as a doughty old soldier, gruff but good-hearted, reluctantly taken in by a brave girl. Even Shaw recycles a legend that when Joan appeared at Baudricourt's keep in Vaucouleurs, the hens stopped laying and the cows ceased giving milk, returning to normal only when Baudricourt agreed to speak to Joan. In fact, Baudricourt was a notorious plunderer and womanizer, and many people were surprised that Joan escaped a meeting with him with her virginity intact.

When Joan finally got to see Baudricourt, she approached him with a straightforward lack of deference, an assumption of equality (she was, after all, sent by her voices) that must have stunned him. At their first meeting, she told him:

I am come before you from my Lord, so that you may tell the dauphin to be of good heart, and not to cease the war against his enemies. Before mid Lent the Lord will give him help. In fact, the kingdom does not belong to the dauphin, but to my Lord. But my Lord wants the dauphin to be made king, and to rule the kingdom. Despite his enemies, the dauphin will be made king; and it is I who will take him to the coronation.[2]

Perhaps the most remarkable word in this extraordinary address is the strongly inflected pronoun "I." So certain was she of the crucial nature of her mission and her fitness to accomplish it that she did not hesitate to predict the success of its outcome. It is this kind of specific and definite prediction that got Joan into trouble when events did not bear out her words.

Baudricourt did not immediately fall into line and grant Joan's requests. At first, he may have thought of keeping her around because she would make good sport for his soldiers. But as a result of her time among his men, more and more of them were drawn to her and pledged their loyalty. So even before she was given the local lord's official sanction, she was beginning to cluster around her men who believed in her because of what must have been the irresistible power of her presence. Jean de Metz, one of the first to join her in Vaucouleurs, said of her: "I had a great trust in what the maid said, and I was on fire with what she said and with a love for her which was, as I believe, a divine love. I believe that she was sent by God."[3] Margaret La Touroulde, widow of the king's receiver general, says of Joan's magnetism: "I heard those who took her to the king say that . . . they thought her presumptuous and their intention was to put her to the proof. But when they had set out to take her, they were ready to do whatever

Joan pleased and were as eager to present her to the King as herself, and that they could not have resisted Joan's will."[4]

Even while she was waiting for Baudricourt, she had begun to have a reputation as a powerful, even magical person. While Baudricourt was dithering, Joan was summoned by Duke Charles of Lorraine, who was in poor health and wanted Joan to cure him. He was hardly an admirable character; he had separated from his wife and kept a mistress by whom he had five bastard children.

Joan told him she could do nothing for his health but that he ought to mend his ways, get rid of his mistress, and take back his wife. Astonishingly, the duke responded to her advice with grateful humility. He gave her four francs and a black horse. Then she asked him to give her his son, the duke of Anjou, and men to take into France, saying that if he did this she would pray for his recovery. The duke agreed.

So Joan returned to Baudricourt with four francs, a black horse, and a noble companion. This moved Baudricourt to meet with her at her lodgings and to bring the curé with him in order to certify that she was not an agent of the devil. It is likely that he was influenced by the growing enthusiasm of the local people, who invoked the prophecies that had prepared Joan's way.

On the first Sunday of Lent, February 13, 1429, Joan set out from Baudricourt's seat at Vaucouleurs to Chinon, the king's headquarters, accompanied by the duke of Anjou, the knights who had attached themselves to her while she was waiting for Baudricourt's support, and the soldiers she had finally been given by him. The 350-mile trip took a re-markably quick eleven days. Joan and her men crossed no fewer than six rivers. They took chances by riding into Bur-gundian territory and even hearing mass publicly at Aux-erre, which was firmly in Burgundian hands. Rumors were already following them. The Bastard of Orléans had sent representatives ahead to the court to discover the truth about them. De la Trémoille may have sent scouts out to ambush Joan and her companions; they were frustrated, and Joan slipped through, in record time, without difficul-ties arising either from the king's supporters or the enemy she had sworn to save him from.

The King's Trick

The story of how Joan first got an audience with the king and then, almost immediately, galvanized him and talked him into sending her to the besieged city of Orléans with an army is a tale that has gained credence not in small part be-cause it is so susceptible to verbal and visual representation.

Joan got into the castle at Chinon relatively easily, and this is in itself extraordinary: It's as if Dorothy got to Oz with no interference from the wicked witch. As if a girl from the boondocks decided to see the president and made her way to the Oval Office without passing through metal detectors. Once she was in the castle, she encountered her first obstacle. Or perhaps, better, her first test.

News of Joan had reached the court, but the king and his council were ambivalent about receiving her. Baudricourt's sponsorship induced the council to abandon their misgivings and allow her to see the king, but not before two days of wrangling about it. When she was given permission to cross the drawbridge, she was insulted by a guard, who said to her: "Isn't that the maid? Jarnidieu (I deny God). If I had her for the night, she wouldn't remain a maid." She later told her confessor that she had answered: "Ha! In God's name, you deny Him when you are so near to death." Within an hour, he had fallen into the water and was drowned.[5]

Having agreed to admit Joan, the council—with or without the king's connivance—decided that the king should disguise himself to see if Joan could see through the ruse and pick him out in a crowd. As befitted the overelaborate protocol of the time, at least three hundred courtiers were assembled in the hall, which was lit by torches. Joan was ushered in and greeted with great ceremony. One of the courtiers—in Shaw's play he is Gilles de Rais, the infamous Bluebeard—was presented to her as the king. But she denied that he was the king and made her way through the crowd to Charles, who was cowering among the courtiers, dressed with purposeful simplicity to conceal his royal identity. Joan fell to her knees before him, saying, according to a witness, "Very noble Lord dauphin, I am come and sent by God to bring succor to you and your kingdom."[6]

This event has been illustrated in such diverse media as the stained glass of Orléans Cathedral, the illustrated children's books by which many of us got our first glimpse of

Joan, and the comedy of Shaw. In it are elements of both ritual and child's play. It involves the kind of testing that depends on proofs irrationally gathered. This may be foreign to the modern juridical mind, but to the essential part of human beings that loves stories, it is not foreign at all, in no small measure because it contains irresistible plot devices. The stranger, the outsider, the innocent, arrives in a milieu for which she is underprepared. The sophisticated city slickers try to trick her, but her native wit defeats them. Abashed and awed, they fall to their knees in front of her.

After this charade, Joan and the dauphin withdrew to a private area. What happened between them is unknowable, but whatever it was seems to have had a transforming effect on Charles, at least temporarily. The depressed and listless young man seemed to become illumined, and new energy was visible in his words and gestures.

The content of Joan and Charles's private conversation has been the subject of an enormous amount of speculation. What did Joan say that had such a galvanizing effect? Most accounts agree that, at minimum, Joan relieved Charles's anxieties about his illegitimacy. Some accounts say that she informed him of the exact words of a prayer he had made in private and in silence, words that were known to no other living soul. Later, under great psychic pressure during her trial, she would claim that an angel had brought Charles a crown from Rheims, but before her death she admitted that she had invented the angel.

The effect that Joan had on the weak and vacillating Charles is a kind of metaphor for her effect on the whole kingdom of France. Like its leader, the realm was demoralized, depressed, and divided against itself. No one had any ideas about how to make anything better; a stagnating and diminishing warfare had sapped people's resolve, their hope and faith. Suddenly, a young, brash creature appeared from the countryside. Her way had been prepared by prophecy: She might well be the virgin whose saving of them had been multiply foretold. She had no doubts, no hesitations. They couldn't find anything to do; therefore, they had nothing to lose. Why not take a chance on her? At least she had an appetite for action.

We can imagine her entering the court like an arrow shot from a doorway, focusing the attention of the bored, dispirited, and purposeless courtiers. All eyes are on the arrow's landing point, waiting for the second when the steel tip pierces the stone surface of the ancient wall, the final moment when the feathered end quivers; then the stillness, until the crowd feels that it can again draw breath.

Quite quickly, Joan seemed to have aroused in Charles an impulse to obey her. She used this in a curious ritual in which she had Charles relinquish the kingdom of France to her.

> One day the Maid asked the king for a present. . . . She asked for the kingdom of France itself. The king, astonished, gave it to her after some hesitation, and the young girl accepted. She even asked that the act be solemnly

drawn up and read by the king's four secretaries. The girl said, showing him to those who were by, "Here you see the poorest knight in his kingdom.". . . And a little later, in the presence of the same notaries, acting as mistress of the kingdom of France, she put [this issue] into the hands of all-powerful God. Then, at the end of some moments more, acting in the name of God, she invested King Charles with the kingdom of France; and she wished a solemn act to be drawn up in writing of all this.[7]

This act shows Joan's highly developed understanding of symbolic action and its power. She is expressing a complex and multifaceted idea: She has power over Charles, but it comes from God, and it is God moving through her who will enable the actions that must, if they are going to be effectual in this world, come from the king. She establishes a tripartite relationship involving herself, the king, and God, with God the fixed point. All things return to the fixed point, God, in the face of whom the relative power difference between king and commoner grow insignificant.

Examination

However inspired Charles may have been by Joan's presence, he was not going to provide her with an army and the resources to keep it going without the support of the Church. He insisted that before he send Joan to Orléans, she be examined by a group of clergymen in order to make sure that her mission was, as she claimed, divinely inspired.

The examining body was made up of seventeen or eighteen members, including the archbishop of Rheims, two other bishops, and the confessors of the king and queen. The records of this interrogation are lost, and the loss marks an important gap in our knowledge of Joan. She was proud, however, of her ability to deal with the learned doctors with equanimity, for she repeatedly suggested at her later trial that her judges refer to the record of Poitiers and stop wasting her time. She was undaunted, even at that first trial, by the gap between the judges' learning and her own. She later bragged that she had said in answer to the judges, "There is more in Our Lord's books than your own," and when she was asked if she believed in God, she said, "Yes, better than you."[8]

It is a sign of the temper of the times that one of the decisive factors in the clerics' decision to approve Joan was their sense that she was the fulfillment of the prophecy that a virgin would come to save France. Fifteenth-century Church doctors had no trouble placing prophecy alongside testimony garnered through legal investigation, and weighing both.

Armed by the King

After she had passed the examination by the learned clerks at Poitiers, Joan went to Tours, where she was given a retinue and had a suit of armor made for her. This delighted her; she was always excited by the accoutrements of knighthood, or of war. At Tours, she was offered a sword, but insisted that the one she needed could be found at St.

Catherine's Church at Fierbois. She said, should the messengers dig behind the altar, they would find a sword concealed there. The priests who were sent on this errand did what they were told and found the sword. When they rubbed it, the rust that had encrusted it immediately fell off, and it was discovered that the sword had five crosses on the hilt and was imprinted with fleurs-de-lis.

Joan claimed that she had never seen the sword and that she was told of its existence by her voices. She had, however, spent a lot of time in the church while she was waiting for a response to her letter to the king at Chinon. Although it is possible that she didn't know of the sword's existence on a conscious level, it is certainly possible that at least unconsciously she had known about it from stories she had heard and forgotten. What is important is Joan's comprehension of the symbolic power of the sword and its method of discovery. She was understood to have prophetic gifts, and the sword was a symbol of her approval by God. Later, it would be understood by the English as a sign of her demonic power.

At Tours, the king also provided payment for the standard she had ordered. This standard became the most famous of her props; the design for the banner was given to her by her voices. The background was white; there was an image of the Trinity, flanked by two angels. It was made of thin linen, and the fabric was embossed with lilies. On the reverse of the banner was an azure shield, supported by two angels, bearing a white dove. The dove held a scroll in its beak, and on the scroll were the words *"de par le Roi de*

Ciel" (of the party of the King of Heaven). These words referred to her divine mandate.

She was preparing for her display, and the preparation called up the part of her genius that brilliantly understood the use of symbols. A few weeks earlier she had appeared before Baudricourt in the traditional red dress of a peasant girl; that dress had been replaced by men's clothing and would not be seen again. But now she would have armor made for her, and she was given a retinue worthy of a prince. She was in command of men whom, for most of her life, she would not have thought of speaking to. Jean d'Aulon was appointed master of her household. Did it seem remarkable to her that she would have a household, to say nothing of one with a master? He would accompany Joan until her capture. She chose a confessor who would also be with her until she was imprisoned, a mendicant friar named Jean Pasquerel, who had met Joan's mother on a pilgrimage.

She set off from Chinon with a long train of horsemen, men-at-arms, wagons, four hundred head of cattle, and priests in front intoning the Veni Creator Spiritus. Her whole retinue consisted of four thousand men. They encamped at the town of Blois, near Orléans. Joan was much concerned with the spiritual state of her soldiers. She insisted that they confess and receive communion. She lectured them, not only on the state of their souls, but on the quality of their language. She forbade them camp followers. They slept in the field the first night, and Joan awoke bruised and weary, unused to the weight of her armor.

CHAPTER III

TRIUMPHANT IN BATTLE, THE KING'S ANOINTER

JOAN HAD IMAGINED that she would ride into Orléans and immediately engage in battle with the English. But the commanders in charge had other plans. She may have thought of herself as a *chef de guerre*, but they thought of her as a mascot, someone who would ride with them, inspire the troops and the citizens, and then, happy to do what she was told by her olders and betters, fall into line. With this in mind, they tricked Joan, who had not paid attention to anything like maps and plans—believing in the strength of her mission and the good faith of her companions-at-arms. Her naïveté is astonishing, but it makes her lack of experience more real, and perhaps justifies some of the professional soldiers' lack of faith in her.

The trick was this: Joan was brought to the south side of the Loire, whereas the English were encamped on the north side. The Bastard of Orléans, who was in charge of the besieged town, had no confidence that Joan's army was strong enough to confront the English. Instead, he wanted to use Joan's forces, not to fight, but to accompany the food and supplies that would relieve the besieged citizens. His plan was to send boats to the side of the river where

Joan was, fill them with supplies, and have them cross the river so that they could enter the one gate of the city that was still open. This plan made great practical sense; the populace could not withstand the siege if it was starving.

We can only guess why the Bastard of Orléans and the other captains didn't tell Joan their plans. Perhaps they didn't take her seriously enough to include her in their councils, or perhaps they understood the intransigence of her personality and knew she'd be dissatisfied with such an undramatic beginning to her military life. Perhaps, when the Bastard of Orléans came across the river to greet Joan, he thought he would be meeting "La Pucelle," a young woman whom he could quickly talk around. Instead, he encountered a furious and frustrated captain with ideas of her own and no inclination to tractability.

The Bastard of Orléans, also known as Dunois, was the illegitimate but acknowledged son of the duke of Orléans, who was in captivity in England. He was in charge of the city and had been interested in Joan since her arrival at Chinon; he'd sent a party there to get the sense of her. It was a mark of his courtesy that he came across the river to Blois to greet her personally.

Joan's initial encounter with Dunois is a comic scene that illuminates her impetuous, hubristic nature. She marched up to him and told him that she had counsel that was of far greater importance than his, and that if he ever did anything like that trick to her again, she'd have his head cut off. "I believe you," he replied. Joan had no hesitation venting her rage in the most aggressive and disrespectful way possible to a man whose blood was at least one-half royal, to the son of her hero (the poetic duke of Orléans), and the ruler of the town she had not yet even seen. But he seems to have shown no resentment of her treatment of him; he always handled her with tact and generosity, and he valued and respected her consistently after their rocky overture.

The city of Orléans is located eighty miles south of Paris on the northern, or right, bank of the Loire. It is currently known as the Newark of France. But in the fifteenth century, its position on the Loire made it of great economic and geographical importance, and the English reckoned that if they could control Orléans they would have control of the surrounding Loire area.

In 1429, Orléans was a city of thirty thousand inhabitants. It was heavily fortified with a complete wall upon which twenty-one cannons were mounted. There were several barred gates guarded with towers and moats and other fortifications outside the walls: Once inside the walls and gates of the city, the inhabitants were safe from their invaders. The English, understanding this, and having failed to pierce the walls with their cannon, decided to capture Orléans through a prolonged siege. When Joan appeared on the scene in April of 1429, the town had been under siege for six months. Both sides seemed hypnotized to the point of paralysis. The English were bogged down because they had not been given the troops or supplies to mount the kind of attack they considered necessary; the French because they were imprisoned in their city.

Dunois convinced Joan that it was necessary for her men to accompany the provisions into Orléans. But even after she agreed to fall in with his plan, there was another problem. The boats were upstream, and the wind prevented them from sailing down to Orléans. It was at this point that Dunois witnessed one of Joan's most important miracles. She told him not to worry about the wind. As soon as she said this, the direction of the wind changed, allowing the boats to proceed.

Joan responded to this nonchalantly: She'd told Dunois not to worry, and she'd meant what she said. Dunois, however, was amazed, and from that time on his faith in Joan was ardent. He persuaded her to cross the river and enter the city with him, leaving her army behind. She was reluctant—she knew the men were eager for battle; but she agreed. They sent the main army back to Blois, taking with them only a task force from the Orléans garrison. Mounted on a white horse, her banner and pennants streaming, Joan triumphantly entered the Burgoyne gate of Orléans at 1 P.M. on April 29. *The Journal of the Siege of Orléans,* an anonymous contemporary chronicle, breathlessly reports the event:

And so she entered Orléans, with the Bastard of Orléans at her left, very richly armed and mounted; afterward came other noble and valiant lords, squires, captains and men at arms, along with the bourgeois of Orléans, carrying many torches and making such joy as if they had seen God Himself descend among them; and not without reason, for they had endured much difficulty, labor, pain, and fear of not being rescued and of losing all their bodies and goods. But they felt already comforted, as though freed of the siege by the divine virtue that they were told resided in that simple Maid, whom they regarded with strong affection, men as much as women and little children. And there was a marvelous crowd pressing to touch her or the horse on which she rode.

The press of the crowd was so great that one of the torchbearers set Joan's pennant aflame. She exhibited extraordinary horsemanship, controlling her terrified horse and putting out the fire. The journal remarks, "She put out the fire as easily as if she had long war expertise; the men at arms considered this a great marvel."[1]

It is remarkable to consider that five months before this event, she had been living in her father's house at Domrémy.

It wasn't till May 4 that she saw her first real fighting. Dunois had told her that Sir John Fastolf, an English commander on whom Shakespeare's Falstaff might be based, was on his way, a day's march from the city. Joan was delighted that at last she would be in the midst of battle. She told Dunois to let her know as soon as Fastolf approached, and went to her room for a rest. A short time later, Joan sprang from her bed and woke her page, telling him that her voices had told her to go against the English. In great agitation, she demanded that she be armed, and she leaped onto her horse. She shouted impatiently for her banner, and it was passed to her through the window. Riding through the town, she heard the news of French blood being shed, which made her weep but did not slow her down.

To her surprise, it was not Sir John Fastolf with whom the French were engaged, but the garrison of a minor fort close to town, a monastery, St. Loup, that the English had taken and fortified. Things were going badly for the French until Joan appeared. Then the English saw the tide turn; they perceived that with Joan at the head of the French they would be defeated. In order to escape, they dressed themselves up in the church vestments they found in the old monastery. Joan appears to have been taken in by this ruse, and stopped the soldiers from slaughtering the people she believed to be priests.

This was the first time the French had succeeded in capturing an English work. It meant that the French could pour supplies and troops into the city by a second gate. Joan insisted that the troops should all be confessed, and decreed that there be no fighting on the next day, May 5, Ascension Day. This reluctance to fight on a feast is important, for it indicates that at this point in her career her military judgment and her religious scruples were coordinated; later, when she was more desperate, they would not be.

After the fall of Fort St. Loup, the English fled to a well-fortified fort or bastille called St. Augustin on the other side of the river. When Joan arrived there, she planted her standard on the edge of the first ditch. But she stepped on a caltrop, a spiked ball, which put her out of the fight. Undiscouraged, the soldiers pushed on and took the fort of St. Augustin. Joan soon returned to her men, made St. Augustin her new headquarters, and prepared for the major Battle of Orléans.

That night the French captains, fearing they didn't have enough troops for a major battle, asked Joan to wait until more help arrived, but she refused and vowed to attack in the morning. Even wounded (it was her first battle wound, though a minor one) she exhibited her characteristic bold courage.

The next morning, May 7, Dunois attacked. Joan charged into the boulevard. About noon, an arrow entered her body, just above her left breast, at exactly the place she had prophesied to her confessor on her way from Chinon to Orléans. She fell back, in shock and in great pain. She wept, despite her foreknowledge of the nature of her wound. It is as though she were surprised, not that she had been struck by an arrow, but that it would hurt. This is a particularly adolescent brand of surprise: the shock at the vulnerability of a body imagined invulnerable. The arrow is said to have penetrated six inches. She is said to have pulled the arrow out herself, but this detail, as well as the detail of the depth of six inches, may be more myth than reality. What is undeniable is that after her wound was dressed with fat (she refused the offer of charms being placed on it) she rested awhile, but joined the fighting again. At 8 P.M., the Bastard wanted to quit for the night. Joan begged him to go on, and she withdrew into a vineyard, where she prayed for a quarter of an hour. She then returned to the battle. Upon seeing her, the soldiers reacted with "great ardor" to the sight of their wounded heroine with them again. But then the trumpet was blown for the retreat. Joan ignored it, disobeying the orders of the other commanders.

Joan was on foot, taking part in an assault that involved crossing the moat and scaling the wall. The soldier who was carrying her standard fainted from exhaustion, and he passed the standard to another soldier, called Le Basque. Jean d'Aulon, the master of her retinue, challenged Le Basque to follow him and charged into the moat, covering himself with his shield to protect himself from stones. Le Basque was slow to follow, and Joan caught up with him before he entered the moat, outraged that a stranger was carrying her standard. She seized it. The soldiers could see the standard, blown by a wind so that it pointed toward the bridge. The soldiers believed, either because Joan had told them or because they had invented the story, that when the standard blew in the direction of the enemy, they would take the wall. The wall *was* taken, and quickly the entire boulevard.

The French had now gained control of the north and south banks of the river and of the bridge, and the English, seeing the handwriting on the wall, lifted the siege on May 8. They collected their army to the north of the town, expecting the French to follow up their victory. Joan gathered her army and went out to confront them. The two armies looked at each other over the field, and then Joan ordered that mass should be said in the field, in fact two masses. Told that the English were marching off, she ordered her troops not to attack, because it was Sunday.

But the English had left Orléans for good, without a major battle, if we understand battle to mean a full-scale confrontation of armies. Their passivity after Joan's arrival is inexplicable; their forces were greater, and they probably could have prevailed. It is precisely this passivity that led people to believe Joan did what she did because of witchcraft, and to accuse her of it at her trial. In a week, Joan had accomplished what well-trained and well-organized captains had not been able to do in six months.

In their joy over the liberation of their city, the bourgeois and the soldiers came together to give thanks in the city's churches. This itself was a major victory: The bourgeois had so feared the undisciplined behavior of the men-at-arms that they were reluctant to have them in the city. But with Joan at their head, all the citizens of Orléans, from the oldest to the youngest, prayed and gave thanks for the Maid who had saved their city. From then on she would be known as the Maid of Orléans.

What are we to make of the Battle of Orléans, and what does it tell us about Joan? Certainly it doesn't suggest that she was a great tactician, as none of the important military decisions were made by her. Some of what she did seems naïve, as when she was duped by the soldiers dressing as priests, and some of the events happened without her bidding, as when Le Basque took her standard and she followed it. What the battle does indicate, indisputably, is her extraordinary physical courage and stamina, her genius for recovery. And it tells us that, both for the French and for the English, she was a presence whose importance and power stemmed not from any traceable action or behavior but from an atmosphere that preceded and surrounded her. So it was not necessary for her to do one thing rather than another; it was necessary only that she be there. And it was necessary that she win. The French needed someone like Joan, someone to break through their paralysis. She broke through and handed them victory. If she had not been victorious, the story would have ended there.

To say that the victory at Orléans was not a victory of Joan's tactics is not to say that if she hadn't behaved with heroic daring the outcome of the battle would have been the same. It is simply to say that the victory, and the reverberations and interpretations that followed it, can be traced to a combination of her hypervisible action and incandescent spirit. This is the point at which myth, symbol, and act collide and create a new essence, when a power is born that is greater than, and different from, any of its separate components. Gift, chance, accident, coincidence. The theological term, of course, is grace.

People who met Joan felt transformed, able to do things they would not have done. This is because they saw her doing things that they had never seen anyone do. And, for a while, their faith seemed justified because she was remarkably successful.

From Strength to Strength:
Jargeau, Meung, Beauregency, and Patay

In order to consolidate her victory at Orléans, Joan had to rout the English from the surrounding towns, particularly Jargeau. On June 10, she approached the town, where the French army had up to this point experienced little success. A supply train was about to reach the English. Once again, Joan's appearance on the scene inspired the troops; they rallied and began a bombardment, bringing down one of the fortified towers. It was at Jargeau that one of Joan's minor miracles took place. She told the duke of Alençon to move, foreseeing that a cannonball was going to hit the spot where he was standing. He obeyed her, moved, and another knight was killed when the cannonball hit. Was this miraculous or just good foresight? If she knew that the ball would hit, why didn't she tell both knights to move? Or did she feel she should use her powers only sparingly, in this case to keep the promise to Alençon's wife that she would keep him safe? A domestic tone enters the scene: a friend's promise to the wife of a friend.

After a battle of three or four hours, the English retreated. During the battle, Joan was knocked off a ladder by a stone, but the helmet she wore protected her from serious injury. Once again, she rose up quickly and went back to work.

When the French succeeded in taking the towns of Meung and Beauregency, the English realized that the Loire campaign was over. So they quit and began to march back toward Paris. The French pursued them. One of the French captains, La Hire, had with him a crack troop, a group of clever scouts and skirmishers (the marines of their day). He decided that the moment to strike was at hand. He didn't wait for the main French army to support him, and he attacked boldly, achieving a quick and complete victory. Talbot (the great English commander idealized by Shakespeare in *Henry VI*) was taken, and the French murdered two thousand soldiers. Only two hundred were taken prisoner—those who were rich enough to afford the possibility of ransom.

Joan arrived only at this point, in the midst of the slaughter. She was shocked by the reality of the human cost of war. She saw a French soldier strike an English prisoner on the head, leaving him bleeding on the ground, close to death. She dismounted and cradled the Englishman's head, hearing his dying confession. This is, to say the least, unusual behavior for a victorious commander.

Joan was given credit for the surrender of the English, though in fact she had taken no part in the fighting.

After Orléans, on to Rheims

It is somewhat surprising that after the victory at Orléans and the small but related victories at Meung, Patay, and Jargeau, she chose not to seize the military moment and press forward on the energetic tide she'd raised but to quit the field for the purpose of anointing the king at Rheims. The explanation for this is Joan's consummate understanding of the power of symbols. Until there was a coronation at Rheims, Charles would be not a king but a dauphin, the son of a dead father, the boy in waiting. The imposition of the mystical oils of Clovis would, she understood, undo the stigma of doubt that had been cast upon him by his mother's suggestion of his illegitimacy. It would also be a vivifying blast through the malaise that had gripped the people and prevented them from moving forward, or moving at all.

But natures do not change quickly, and Charles, whose dominant characteristics included ambivalent vacillation, resisted Joan's attempts to get him crowned. When she went to de la Trémoille's castle at Sully to see him, he told her to calm down and not trouble herself so much for him. She wept and told him, "Have no doubt you will gain your whole kingdom and soon be crowned."[2] Part of his hesitation might have come from the fact that he was living as de la Trémoille's guest, and the party of de la Trémoille was never on Joan's side; it is likely that he would have warned Charles that he had created a monster who would end up devouring him.

Joan was sulky and impatient at the king's delay, and her frustration led her to arrogate certain powers to herself that were not properly hers. She had the duke of Alençon, her favorite noble companion, sound the trumpets and mount his horse. She told him, "It is time to go to the gentle king Charles to put him on his road to his coronation at Rheims."[3] She wrote a letter to the citizens of the town of Tournai, taking credit for all the military successes the army had achieved and telling them, "I pray and require you to be ready to come to the anointing of the gentle King Charles at Rheims where we shall be soon, and to come into our presence when you know that we approach."[4] Charles, however, had given her no specific promise or specific date.

But even his pusillanimous temperament was not unmoved by Joan's great popular success. Great numbers of men joined her ranks, swelling the army to proportions that were unknown before her arrival. This worried Charles, since he knew he didn't have the resources to pay all these soldiers (later on these men would suffer greatly from being improperly provisioned), but, by the end of June, he was prepared to move on to Rheims.

The cities on the way to Rheims were Burgundian in sympathy, and they did not willingly open their doors to Charles. Part of their reluctance was that they didn't want the notoriously ill-disciplined French troops within their walls. The city of Troyes greeted Joan and Charles with cannon shots from the garrison, but the French forces outnumbered them. The bishop of Troyes came out to see

Charles, urging him to wait while he negotiated with the townspeople.

The army was nearly starving, and it was only a fortuitous coincidence that saved them. Living in Troyes at the time was Joan's old friend the apocalyptic preacher Brother Richard, who was staunchly loyal to the French. The army was saved from starvation because of the townspeople's misunderstanding of one of his sermons the previous year. He had said, "Sow, good people, sow plenty of beans, for he who should come will come very soon."[5] What he meant was the Antichrist, but the people understood that "he who should come" as Charles. The soldiers ate the beans and survived.

Even after the army was fed, there was the problem of persuading the people of Troyes to open their doors to Charles. Neither Brother Richard nor the bishop was succeeding. Joan was allowed to present her case. She knelt to the king and the bishop of Rheims and said, "Noble Dauphin, command young people to come and besiege the city of Troyes and drag out your debates no longer for in God's name, within three days I will lead you into the city of Troyes, by love, force, or courage, and that false Burgundy will be quite thunderstruck."[6]

Once again, Joan's certainty and strength of tone prevailed, and the bishop allowed her to start a siege if she could guarantee that she would be successful in six days. She guaranteed it, and made such good strategic decisions about the placement of artillery that the military men were astonished.

When she began her attack, the citizens of Troyes panicked, and within a day they were bargaining with the king, agreeing to terms that were favorable to him. Joan entered the city to prepare for the king's ceremonial entry, placing archers to line the streets. She rode beside the king, carrying the standard, accompanied by the principal captains in all their finery. In addition to planning and taking part in the procession, Joan agreed to act as godmother to a baby who was born that day.

There are two conflicting reports on Joan at Troyes. An Anglo-Burgundian soldier said she was "the simplest thing he ever saw, and in what she did there was neither rhyme nor reason, any more than the stupidest thing he ever saw. He thought that she was not to be compared with Madame d'Or, the female jester of the duke of Burgundy, who was famous for her long blonde hair."[7]

Responding to Joan very differently, other eyewitnesses claimed that they had seen thousands of white butterflies flying around her standard. The discrepancy is an early example of the range of response Joan's complex character could elicit.

There was feeling among the citizenry of Rheims that they should wait to see what the duke of Burgundy had to offer them before they opened their gates to Charles. So there was some delay in his entering the city. He finally entered the city on a Saturday; the customary day for coronation was Sunday. This meant that the ceremony had to be planned quickly, and as a result it lacked some of the grandeur that had always gone with the coronation of the kings of France. The habitual coronation regalia was unavailable, since it was kept at St.-Denis, near Paris, still in English hands. Nevertheless, at 3 A.M., Charles entered the cathedral for the traditional vigil before he was knighted, and at nine the ritual began.

Notre Dame de Rheims would have been the second great cathedral Joan had seen. She had prayed for assistance at St. Croix d'Orléans and then triumphantly offered thanks there for her great victory. Orléans was, however, a minor structure compared to Notre Dame de Rheims, one of the great architectural marvels of the world. It is unlikely, though, that Joan's attention would have traveled to the façade or to any of the other twenty-three hundred major statues, celebrating everything from the visitation of the Virgin to the slaughtering of a pig during harvest time. She would probably not have noticed the famous stone angel at the church door, that enigmatic smiler, ironic, accepting, merciful but commonsensical, a face that both mirrors Joan's best qualities and is bemused by the hint of extremism that she represents. But Joan's sense of drama must have been aroused by the majestic vaulting of the great nave down which she walked, her armor covered with a tunic of white silk, the only female in the procession, the only member neither clerical nor noble, and the youngest of them all.

There were important irregularities in the ceremony, which mirrored contemporary political irregularities. Of the twelve peers of France who were supposed to stand forward for the king, most sent substitutes. One of the absent peers was the duke of Burgundy, Charles's sworn enemy. Another missing person was Pierre Cauchon, archbishop of Beauvais, the strongest French supporter of the English and the future presider at Joan's trial.

But the most striking anomaly was the presence of a young woman, a commoner. Throughout the whole ceremony, Joan stood beside the king, holding her standard. At her trial, Joan was asked why her standard was unfurled in the cathedral when those of the other captains were excluded. With her characteristic pride she answered, "It had borne the burden, and it was right that it should have the honor."[8]

Joan's response to the coronation was, again characteristically, emotionally expressive. She knelt, embraced the king's knees, and wept, assuring the king that he was indeed king of France now and that her prophecies had been fulfilled.

Despite the short notice of the coronation, the city was overwhelmed with crowds; the vines planted in the surrounding fields were trampled by the throngs of horses. Among the visitors were Joan's father and her uncle, Durand Laxault, who had been her first supporter. They lingered for two months in the city, enjoying what must have been the only holiday of their lives.

On the day of the coronation, Joan found time to dictate a letter to the duke of Burgundy. She addressed him with taunting arrogance. She told him that, as the king's vassal, he should know that his duty was to make a lasting peace with the king and that if he wanted to go to war, he should fight the Saracens. She threatened him:

> You will not win a battle against the loyal Frenchman, and all those who make war against the holy realm of France, make war against King Jesus, king of heaven, and all the world, my rightful and sovereign Lord.[9]

The King Is Crowned; Then What?

Joan left the city of Rheims at the height of her power and success. She suggested that, her mission to crown the king having been completed, it was time for her to go home to Domrémy. Had she followed this impulse, she would have experienced only success and might have died in bed, a local legend. But she wanted to go on to Paris, and she believed that the king wanted the same thing.

Clearly, however, she and Charles had different goals. It is difficult to understand Charles favorably or, rather, to put him in any kind of nonexculpatory light. History has not been kind to him; it has painted him as a coward and a dupe. Certainly his behavior toward Joan is an example of crashing disloyalty; as soon as he was crowned, he seemed, at best, to lose interest in the woman who had crowned him. Many Joanolaters feel that he undermined her best efforts. Certainly he was invisible when she was in her most dire need.

From a political standpoint, however, Charles was, in

the long run, a success. He died with the French crown still on his head, ruling over a united France. His enemies had lost their sway, and if he betrayed Joan in life, he saw to it—for his own reasons, of course—that her name was, in death, glorified.

To make a rather weak defense for him, the Joan whom he thought he was signing up at Chinon was not the person he had to confront after the coronation. At the center of a court paralyzed by a consistent low-grade depression, he was presented with a boy/girl on horseback who assured him of his legitimacy and whose energy and faith raised his dormant hopes. In equipping her and sending her to his demoralized army, he might have thought he was investing in a curiosity, someone who would be of temporary use and then disappear—or go home.

But the victory in Orléans and the coronation strengthened Joan's position as a figure whose source of power was only partly mythical. People flocked to her; she was a legend who prompted popular action. Because of her, Charles had a larger army than ever, and one his scant resources could hardly support. Having triumphed at Orléans, Joan was convinced of her own status as *chef de guerre* and of her right to take her place beside the great captains of the French army. She did not remain in the place Charles had wanted her to occupy.

Charles and Joan illustrate a phenomenon that occurs when young women want to move from the realm of the symbolic, where male imagination has placed them, to the realm of the actual, where they want to be. A girl can be an ornament, but if she wants to act rather than be looked at, if she wants scope and autonomy rather than the static fate of the regarded, even the well-regarded, object, she becomes dangerous. Joan had not changed; she was, rather, misread. And for this misreading, for which she was not responsible except, perhaps, in failing to understand that other people lacked her courage and her tenacity of vision, she would be punished, at the very least by a loss of favor.

It seems that the appetite for combat that Charles displayed when he equipped Joan to go to Orléans was quickly sated. Perhaps he only wanted a token victory; in any case, he certainly did not share Joan's unequivocal determination to take Paris by force. Charles associated Paris with bad things; in 1418 he had escaped with his life when the Burgundians took over the city. It was a devastating defeat, a massacre in which nearly five thousand people were killed.

Charles understood, perhaps better than Joan, the shaky situation of his finances and the consequences this would have on an army for which he would have to provide. A move to capture Paris would require a major capital outlay, and capital was what he did not have. This was one motivation for his desire to negotiate with Burgundy rather than to confront him militarily. His source of wealth, de la Trémoille, was of the party of negotiation; certainly this would have influenced Charles. And it would make sense that he might have felt some residual guilt in the murder of the father of the duke of Burgundy, a guilt that could have diluted his ardor for full-scale pursuit.

None of these considerations held any sway with Joan.

She seems not to have cared, or not to have noticed, that she was pursuing a policy that her beloved king did not wholeheartedly support. For her, the capture of Paris had a mystical significance. It was part of her three-point plan—she would take Orléans, crown the king, and march to Paris—a plan that had been spelled out for her by her voices. She knew what she wanted, and Charles wasn't sure. His own desires weren't clear to him; the problems with Joan's policy were.

Not only could he see the problems with her plans; her attitude was also troubling. She wasn't showing the deference to him and his advisers that her emotional protestations and gestures of loyalty might have suggested. Her letter to the duke of Burgundy on the day of coronation was written without consultation with Charles and his counselors and in a tone bound to make negotiation more difficult. Joan's understanding of the shape that her loyalty to the king would have to take seems a bit ill considered, half-digested, immature. A large part of loyalty to a sovereign must include obeying his wishes and making him look good. This seems never to have entered Joan's mind. She knew what needed to be done; he was the king, but she had her voices.

Even as Charles was making a triumphal march toward Paris, he was negotiating with Burgundy. Less than a month after he was crowned in Rheims, he had signed a two-week truce with Burgundy, on terms that were, according to Joan's supporters, far from favorable to him. Joan's response to this truce in her letter to the citizens of

Rheims reveals her unhappiness with Charles's policy and her inability to do anything about it. It is a sign at once of her undiminished sense of her own authority and her frustration at being unable to act upon it.

> It is true that the king has made a truce with the Duke of Burgundy to last for fifteen days, by which the duke must surrender the city to him peaceably at the end of the fifteenth day. However do not be surprised if I do not enter Paris as soon as this, since I am not content with the truce which has been thus made and do not know if I will keep it. But if I do keep it, it will be only for the sake of the king's honor. Yet they will not abuse the blood royal, for I will hold and keep together the king's army, so as to be ready at the end of the fifteenth of the said days, if they do not make peace.[10]

This is a remarkable document from a subject who had only a few days before knelt and embraced the king's knees. Her words, and their tone, make clear that she had no hesitation in publicly expressing her problems with royal policy. Obviously, this would never be a wise move for someone whose position was dependent on the favor of the king. But the wisdom of the world was something that was of no interest to Joan; she seems to have lacked any impulse toward self-protection or calculation of a policy that would safeguard her position.

The letter is also a sign of Joan's pleasure in combat and her focus on military action as the important way changes in policy are made. It makes more poignant the question of what could have happened to Joan if she hadn't been burned; life in Domrémy would have been impossible for her. Perhaps for her, as well as for our collective imagination, it was preferable that she go out in a blaze. Her unhappiness living in Charles's court in the months when he wouldn't allow her to go into battle suggests that she could only be herself leading men into battle; any other life would be insufficient.

Joan's radical independence was difficult enough for Charles to bear when Joan was having success in battle. But then she began to lose. Because he had no real personal loyalty to her, because he was interested in her only in what she could represent, when her representations failed to be of use to him, she ceased to exist as important or, perhaps, even real.

Joan's relations with Charles are a metaphor for the problem she could not resolve—the conflict between the mythical and the actual. It is as if she were riding in a chariot drawn by two horses. The chariot could move with breathtaking speed and sureness as long as the two horses kept the same pace, as they did at Orléans, when the myth of the conquering virgin came together with the actuality of the victorious soldier. Her army, successful and well fed, could love both the idea of her and what she had accomplished. But when the gap began to widen between what she suggested or promised and what she could achieve, when the actual outran the mythical, the chariot was overturned, with no possible outcome but disaster.

·   ·   ·

Charles's policy was responsible for his ultimate success twenty-five years after Joan's death, but it couldn't have happened without her. Shortly after Joan's death, the duke of Burgundy seems to have become favorably disposed toward seeking peace, a process that was concluded successfully four years later. An assassination attempt on the life of de la Trémoille, Joan's enemy, was frustrated because the sword couldn't penetrate his flesh, but it ended his appetite for court life. With him gone, the popular desire for military action was no longer thwarted. In 1437, Charles triumphantly entered Paris, fulfilling Joan's 1431 prophecy that this would happen within seven years.

But just as he could not have succeeded without Joan, Charles, given his character and resources, could not accommodate this difficult figure. There was probably no way—five hundred years later, there may still be no way—to make a place for a headstrong woman, full of faith, utterly lacking in self-interest, a little weak on policy but strong on popular appeal. In the relationship of Charles and Joan, we see played out the conflict between the visionary and the practical politician. The latter might need the former, but only for a while. In the long run, she's more a problem than an asset.

In all the months she spent in prison, Joan received no word from Charles. What is remarkable is that she never seemed to resent this; she died believing him worthy of her love and her devotion, the anointed of the Lord, anointed with the sacred oil of Clovis that shone on his temples because of her.

CHAPTER IV

WHAT KIND OF WARRIOR,
WHAT KIND OF DEFEAT?

After the Coronation

IT WOULD SEEM that a grateful Charles would have given the woman who was responsible for his coronation anything she wanted. But he was reluctant to wage war and particularly susceptible to the advice of de la Trémoille, who strongly favored a diplomatic solution. At the very time that Joan had no desire but to press forward for Paris, Charles was negotiating a truce with the duke of Burgundy, which was to last for fifteen days. Joan was suspicious of this truce, and rightly so. Burgundy never had any intention of giving Paris over to Charles; he had merely gained a crucial two weeks for himself, allowing the English to prepare to fight against Charles's army.

The duke of Bedford, the English regent in France, having plenty of time to prepare, seems to have wanted to challenge the French. He addressed an insulting letter to Charles on August 7, denying his legitimacy, accusing him of the murder of John the Fearless, and calling Joan "that disorderly woman dressed as a man."[1] But neither the French nor the English seemed really to want to fight, and not much of consequence happened in this period, except that de la Trémoille fell off his horse and was nearly taken prisoner because he was so heavy he couldn't get himself up off the ground. In the end, the two armies withdrew from one another, in the words of Vita Sackville-West, "like two dogs who have stalked round and round one another growling with raised hackles, but who have finally decided on discretion rather than valor."[2]

Bedford went back to Paris, and Charles was persuaded to advance toward Compiègne. It seemed, for a time, as if Joan had regained her influence with him. She and the duke of Alençon proceeded to St.-Denis, near Paris, and the king sulkily removed himself.

Throughout the end of August there were skirmishes but no serious attacks. Then came September 8, an important date because it was the Feast of the Nativity of the Virgin. On Ascension Day, only a few months before, when Joan was powerful and victorious, she had refused to allow her troops to attack on a holy day. Now, stymied and frustrated, she ordered the attack. But she seems to have lost the ability to rally and inspire the troops. The French captains fought halfheartedly, and Joan's army suffered its first important reverse since Orléans.

An arrow penetrated Joan's thigh, and she was, against her protestations, removed from the field. Charles used her wound as an excuse to give up the fight and ordered Joan to withdraw and meet him at St.-Denis. Inexplicably—or perhaps his reluctance that Joan should capture and disturb his negotiations with Burgundy explains it—Charles had a bridge that the duke of Alençon had thrown up across the Seine burned. Perhaps he didn't trust Joan to obey his orders.

Time, Symbol, Substance

Of the poignancies surrounding Joan, the brevity of everything concerning her is perhaps the greatest. There is the brevity of her life as a whole: nineteen years. But it is astonishing to contemplate the fact that her success lasted, by the most generous interpretation, nine months (if you start calculating at Vaucouleurs) or, alternatively, less than five, if you begin counting at Orléans.

Stagnancy

Joan's army was disbanded at the end of October. The docility with which she accepted this decline is surprising, given her fiery nature. Instead of going home to tend her sheep, as she'd said she wanted to do after the coronation, Joan traveled with the court for most of the fall. There could hardly have been a worse situation for her. It is dispiriting to imagine her trapped with the frivolous, luxury-loving but bankrupt courtiers, so inimical to everything she stood for and admired. Temperamentally, she was ill suited for the idleness of court life. She couldn't wait to return to battle, and her chronic impatience might have caused her to decide unwisely. Moreover, perhaps her constant urging made the court so anxious to get rid of her that they'd do whatever she said rather than put up with her presence.

It must have been a relief to her when the king authorized her to take the town of La Charité, fifty or so miles to the south of Orléans, which was "owned" by the warlord Perinnet Gressart. The first step was to take the small town of St. Pierre Le Moutier. There, greeted by a small force of English, she experienced another success, which she attributed to the fifty thousand she had behind her, either a reference to the heavenly host or a moment of madness, depending on your interpretation. In fact, the number of men she had with her was very small.

Her fifty thousand let her down, however, at La Charité. It was a long and unsuccessful siege, and in November she had to return to court a failure. A contemporary chronicler places the blame on the king because he had sent an army of mercenaries and then failed to pay them.

Joan understood herself as a symbolic figure, and she understood the symbolic nature of her entire enterprise. But a symbol, to be effective, must be unambiguous and without contradictions. As Max Weber says of the charismatic hero: "The continued existence of charismatic authority is, by its very nature, characteristically unstable. . . . those who entrust themselves to him must prosper. If they do not, he is not the master."[3]

Joan symbolized victorious rescue; when she started to lose, her symbolism lost its potency. For a while, Joan could inspire the soldiers to fight against ridiculous odds, unpaid and underfed. But not forever. By the time the army was marching to Auxerre from Rheims, and certainly on its march to Paris, the poorly provisioned and unpaid soldiers had deserted in large numbers. Charles was unable or unwilling to give Joan the resources she needed to continue a difficult campaign; she couldn't make it work on air forever.

Her defeats, then, occurred when symbolic action was insufficient, when the reality drowned the image and the dream. When Joan actually began making tactical decisions—in Paris and at La Charité, for example—her lack of experience, her native impetuousness, betrayed her. She was not a professional, and there is something to be said for professionalism as a way of getting through the long haul.

Last Battles and Capture:
The Limits of Audacity and Ardor

Joan stayed with the court until March of 1430. By this point, even Charles had to admit that Joan was right: Burgundy was not bargaining in good faith, and peace would only be won "at the point of a lance." She was sent to Melun, which turned its allegiance from Burgundy to France at the sight of Joan: an outcome which must have reassured her that she hadn't lost her touch. It was at Melun, though, where St. Catherine and St. Margaret warned her that she would be captured before midsummer. Despite what must have been her distress at her voices' first discouraging words, she moved on to Lagny, where another miracle occurred. A baby believed dead was brought to her. "As black as my cloak," she reported at her trial. When she took the baby in her arms, he drew breath and lived long enough to be baptized before he died. It was at Lagny that she captured the Burgundian sympathizer d'Arras, a disastrous figure in her history.

After his capture, Franquet d'Arras was offered quarter and his ransom was fixed. She had intended to exchange him for another man, but then discovered that the other man had been executed. So, going back on her agreement to give Franquet d'Arras up for ransom, she brought him to trial. He was a bad character; his trial lasted fifteen days; he confessed to being a murderer, a thief, and a traitor. He was decapitated.

According to the rules of chivalry, his bad character didn't excuse what Joan did, nor did the death of the prisoner for whom he was meant to be exchanged. Joan had given her promise; the prisoner had been given quarter, ransom had been arranged. She went back on her word, her *parole*, sacred to the ideal of chivalry. Would she have made such an unwise and indeed brutal error if she had been in a time of greater success, more sure of herself, if she'd had the knights she fought beside at Orléans to coach her?

Charles understood that in order to rout the English and Burgundians, a victory on a scale greater than Orléans would be required. It was obvious that the English and Burgundians would join forces and that they would need to capture Compiègne, a town a few miles northeast of Paris that had refused to be handed over to the Burgundians, even though Charles was willing to give it up. If it remained in French hands, it would be a strong position from which to threaten Paris.

In May, events at the town of Soissons indicated that Joan had lost her authority. She wanted to cross the bridge of Soissons to outflank the Burgundians, but the captain of the town, who was in the process of literally selling the town to the Burgundians, would not let her and her men in. Joan's army slept in the field that night and was broken up the next day because the men could not be fed.

She contemplated taking Compiègne with only two or three hundred men. The Burgundian army consisted of six thousand. Some of her companions thought an encounter would be foolhardy; she responded with her usual bravado: "By my staff, we are enough. I will go and see my good friends at Compiègne."[4] This bravado had worked at Orléans, but she was then at the height of her power, the army was comparatively well fed, and, more important, it was ready to be inspired by her. She rode from Soissons to Compiègne all night and arrived at five in the morning, exhausted. But she insisted on making a sortie by 5 P.M.: another instance of her tirelessness, which in the past had worked well.

At first, she seemed to take the Burgundians by surprise. She approached the field on a light-dapple-gray horse, "very beautiful and fiery."[5] Her standards were flying. She had the bells rung. The first rush brought Joan into the Burgundian camp, where the soldiers were mostly disarmed and resting. She was lucky for a time, but only for a time. From a hilltop, the daunting Burgundian captain Jean de Luxembourg spotted Joan and had time to order his troops to meet her. Despite this, Joan, desperately and perhaps foolishly, made two further assaults, with at least some success. But then Luxembourg's men were joined by the duke of Burgundy's and the English. Her followers begged her to retreat to Compiègne, and she responded with anger. "Their discomfiture depends only on you. Think only of falling upon them."[6] It was the sort of challenge to which her men would have risen in the past, but she could not rally them now; either her authority had dissipated or the odds really were impossible.

Eventually, the English cut off Joan's line of retreat. Her men fled toward the safety of the town. Joan found herself trapped. The governor of the town, seeing the army so closely pursued by the enemy, drew up the drawbridge to keep the town in safety. Joan could not get into the town. She was entirely cut off. She fought gallantly, as gallantly as she had done at any point. But she was stuck in the boggy ground: a metaphor, perhaps, for the entropy from which she was trying to extricate her beloved France. The bog overwhelmed her, and a Picard archer seized her by the flaps of her beautiful gold and scarlet surcoat and pulled her ignominiously from her horse. Here another metaphor seems to hold sway. She was caught by the garment that she wore out of a love of display; she was pulled from the "fiery spirited horse," and it was on horseback that she presented her most inspiring version of herself.

·   ·   ·

She was taken into custody by the duke of Luxembourg and imprisoned at the fortress of Beaulieu. The rumor is that the duke of Burgundy arrived that night to have a look at her. Had he been able to talk one of his employees, the court painter Rogier van der Weyden, into accompanying him, we might have a contemporary portrait of Joan by a master. But the duke came unaccompanied. That very evening, he wrote a letter to the inhabitants of St. Quentin, saying her capture was of the greatest importance, because it will expose "the error and foolish credulity of those who have been well disposed and favorable towards the doings of this woman."

For the rest of her life, Joan was no longer a warrior but a prisoner. She would never be free again.

Was She a Knight, and What Kind of Knight Was She?

It would have been customary to make some attempt to ransom a warrior of her caliber, who would, of course, have been a knight. But no attempt was made by Charles or the French, and the Burgundians quickly gave up the hope that they would make money off their capture of Joan. The protections of chivalry seem to have dropped off her as quickly as her armor.

But was she ever really a knight? She refused ennoblement for herself, asking for it only for her brothers. Is it possible to say, then, that she fought like a knight but otherwise didn't behave like one?

This is not entirely surprising. Boys began their knightly training at the age of four. Joan started and finished this education in a matter of weeks. Perhaps because of this, like much else about her, Joan's relationship to chivalry and its code was erratic. She would probably have heard chivalric romances recited in Domrémy; Lorraine, her home province, was particularly devoted to the chivalric ideal. The crusader Godfrey of Boullion was a local hero in the area around Domrémy. He had sold his estates to raise funds for the crusade; he was elected king of Jerusalem but refused the title, preferring instead the saintly moniker Advocatus Sancti Sepulchri, defender of the Holy Sepulchre.

Joan may have admired some aspects of the chivalric idea, but her nature was unsuited to most of the ways it was expressed in her day. In *The Waning of the Middle Ages*, Johan Huizinga characterizes the fourteenth and fifteenth centuries as an age weighted down by its devotion to embellishment and an increasingly and eventually debilitatingly complex set of behaviors. Eventually the excess capsized the medieval boat and sent passengers swimming (although not without the water wings of the past) to the Renaissance. The time could find its metaphor in shoes whose points were so long that the people wearing them tripped over them; chains had to be attached to the points so that the noble wearer could hold on to them. Headdresses were so high and heavy that they interfered with movement; doorways had to be raised to accommodate them. The multiplication of religious devotions erased effective piety. Literary conventions were so otiose that they strangled poetic expression. In opposition to all this, Joan consistently employed direct, plain speech and was devoted to practical outcomes. She identified with the aspects of chivalry that were most active: heroic self-sacrifice, forgetfulness of self to save others or in the defense of a great cause. But she had no time for forms or ceremonies that would slow her down.

She was a master of symbols, but the symbols she chose were simple and easily read. Her banner bore the sign of the fleur-de-lis and the words "Jesus Maria." What more straightforward evocation of religion and patriotism would be possible? Her symbolism was accessible to all, nobles and simples alike; it had nothing to do with knightly culture except that it was used in the service of war: Her pennant was a practical beacon as much as a sign. Her acts of chivalric generosity were usually simple and effective. She provided wine for the wedding of the daughter of the man who designed her standard; she made sure that Domrémy was exempt from taxes. Even her gifts were modest: She sent to the widow of her ideal knight, Guy de Laval, nothing more complex or costly than a plain gold ring.

Her attachment to knighthood was practical: Warfare was the only way she could imagine France's restoration, and war was waged by knights. She was not devoted to the ceremonies of knighthood—she ate very little, and without formality. She had no interest in courtship or the conventions of courtly love. Her interest was in the active life of battle. She was fond of knightly finery and accused of sumptuary vanity during her trial, but she never allowed her clothing to get in the way of its function. Or she did, once and tragically, when she was caught by the tails of her gold surcoat and dragged by them from her horse.

When some aspect of chivalry got in her way, she disregarded it. She seemed unattached to custom and tradition except when she could use it to further her military and political goals. She had no sympathy with the kind of empty gesture embodied in the actions of the English captain Suffolk when he was captured at Jargeau by an Auvergnat squire named Regnault, eager for the ransom that a great man like Suffolk would call forth. Suffolk asked if Regnault was a gentleman. Regnault said he was, whereupon Suffolk asked if he was a knight. Regnault answered that he was not. So Suffolk, unwilling to be taken prisoner by a man of a lower rank, knighted him on the spot, and then surrendered to him. Her habit of mind insisted that the thing is more important than the idea of the thing, the result more important than the gesture. In this she is far from the idealized abstraction that characterized the code of chivalry in the age in which she lived. She was a soldier and an effective mass communicator. In her organization of the values by which she decided her actions, she remained the "cowgirl" that her English enemies accused her of being.

She shouldn't have been able to do what she did. Ride at the head of an army. Lead men into battle. Be victorious. A year earlier, she hadn't known how to ride a horse. She'd practiced by riding on the backs of her father's cattle. She taught herself to ride in the few weeks she lived at

Neufchâtel, while she worked at the tavern of La Rousse, when her family was fleeing the Burgundians. She had never worn armor, and the armor weighed sixty pounds—a much heavier burden on the body of a short woman than on the body of a tall man. She did what she did beside men who had trained for it since early childhood. She had never studied tactics. She had never even seen a battle. But she knew she was a warrior; her voices told her she would lead men to victory. She harbored no doubts.

How is such achievement explicable? Joan reached a level both of physical prowess and of courage that was enormously against all odds. Can this kind of achievement properly be called miraculous? Or is it just an event that is very unlikely? What is the relationship between what we are able to comfortably call genius and what we are unwilling to call miraculous?

She was fearless and tireless, and her courage never flagged. Among men at arms, she was her happiest.

It couldn't last, at least in part because she had never been officially ennobled.

Her Violence: "A Bloodthirsty Wench"?

Joan's voices led her not into a convent or to a hermit's cave but into battle. Her métier was violence. Yet her attitude toward the realities of war—shed blood, torn flesh—is difficult to pin down. Like so much else about her, it seems contradictory and uneven. There is the girl who weeps at both French and English carnage, who cradles an English soldier's head in her lap and hears his confession before he dies. There is the accused prisoner who swears that she never killed a man. Can that be possible? And if it is, what does it say about her as a warrior? Marina Warner questions whether her role as warrior, given this evidence, was more ceremonial than actual.

What did she like about war? Or about going to battle? When questioned during her trial, she said she loved "her standard forty times more than her sword."[7] She herself bore her standard during an attack, she said, in order to avoid killing anyone. And she added that she had never killed anyone at all. But she bragged that her sword was good for giving (in different translations) "good slashes," "good buffets and good swipes," or "good clouts." Is it possible that she could have slashed, buffeted, swiped, and clouted men who were wielding their swords at her and have killed no one? Possible but not likely; and anyone with pride in her sword knows what it's capable of and why she has it in her hand.

What does it mean to call yourself a *chef de guerre* but to arrange things so that you never have to kill anyone? What did she think she was about? What did she think a soldier's business was? Soldiers are, after all, in the killing business, not in the standard-bearing business.

So was it that she liked action and the company of men of action, that she liked danger and the escape from and survival of it? That she liked being obeyed, that she liked the attention that came with being in armor, carrying a standard at the head of a group of soldiers? That she loved display and the elaborate dress that such display required and was expert in the art of both? She made herself, by her white armor, her cloak in the Orléans colors, her short gold jacket, desirably visible, and the sight of her inspired her troops. She reveled in this power. Is she different from other soldiers in forgetting that the enterprise that allows her to dress up and to parade involves butchery?

Was she so intent upon the idea of a France united under Charles, the French king, that she forgot the bloodshed involved? It is important to remember that fifteenth-century warfare was much less distant and abstract than its modern counterpart. Vita Sackville-West notes that, in comparison to modern warfare,

> the personal element was much more dominant for each man concerned. He was in no danger of being suddenly blown to bits by an unseen gun a couple of miles away. . . . The men who ordered his fate were not vague tiny figures sticking pins into a map at a distant GSQ. On the other hand, he was quite likely to be tumbled backwards off a ladder by the fist of an enemy thrust against his face, and the men in the highest positions of command were equally likely to be fighting by his side, as sweaty, gasping and exhausted as he.[8]

Was she not like other soldiers in their necessary habit of radical compartmentalization, in her case in having to put away the girl who wept when she held the dying Englishman's head in order to see him as the enemy? She had no belief in diplomatic negotiations; she was impatient to the point of fury at the idea of truces and treaties with either English or Burgundians. She rejected the English offer to leave Jargeau if given a little time; eleven hundred men were killed that day. When she put Franquet d'Arras to death, five hundred of his men went with him. If she had gone along with her deal to exchange him, they, too, could have been spared.

Joan's beloved sword, the one found behind the altar of St. Catherine's Church at Fierbois, was rendered useless when she broke it over the back of a camp follower and it split in two. This put Charles into a panic; he took it as a bad omen that the sword, which had been read as a sign of divine approbation, had been shattered by Joan's rage at a common whore.

Boasting and Tears

Joan's relationship to violence may be ambiguous, but there is one quality traditionally associated with soldiers that no one would hesitate in attributing to her. She was boastful.

Just after she had been examined at Poitiers, before she had done anything to prove her right to authority, she wrote to Bedford, the English regent, and to Suffolk and Talbot, the English high command. It was their first contact with her and the first thing they had heard about her except by rumor. The bravado of her tone is extravagant to the point of delusion:

Acknowledge the summons of the king of heaven. Render to the Maid here sent by God the king of Heaven, the keys of all the good towns which you have taken and violated in France. She is here come by God's will to reclaim the blood royal. She is very ready to make peace, if you will acknowledge her to be right, provided that France you return, and pay for having held it. And your archers, companions of war, men-at-arms and others who are before the town of Orléans, go away into your country, by God. And if so be not done, expect news of the Maid who will come to see you shortly to your very great injury. King of England, if you do not so, I am chief-of-war and in whatever place I attain your people in France, I will make them quit it willy-nilly. And if they will not obey, I will have them all slain; I am here sent by God, the King of Heaven, body for body, to drive you out of all France. And if they will obey I will be merciful to them. And be not of another opinion, for you will not hold the Kingdom of France from God, the King of Heaven, Son of St. Mary, but will hold it for King Charles, the rightful heir, for God, the King of Heaven so wills it, and that is revealed to him by the maid who will enter into Paris with a goodly company. If you will not believe the news conveyed by God and the Maid, in what place soever we will find you, we shall strike into it and there make such a great *hahay* that none so great has been in France for a thousand years, if you yield not to right. And believe firmly that the King of Heaven will send greater strength to the Maid than you will be able to bring up against her and her good men-at-arms, and when it comes to blows, it will be seen who has the better right of the God of Heaven. You, Duke of Bedford, the Maid prays and requires of you that you cause no more destruction to be done. If you grant her right, still may you come into her company there where the French shall do the greatest feat of arms which ever was done in Christianity. And make answer if you wish to make peace in the city of Orleans. And if you make it not, you shall shortly remember it, to your very great injury.[9]

The tone of this letter is remarkable in several ways. First, for its confident aggressiveness, particularly considering that it was dictated by an eighteen-year-old illiterate peasant and sent to the regent of England and his commanders. A sign of this confidence, and the mastery and understanding it provided Joan, is her imposition of the term "the Maid." Her using the term "La Pucelle," the Maid, was an inspired stroke. It put her into a mythical context; it erased the stigma of her social inferiority and transformed her from upstart to icon.

Stylistically, the letter has none of the elegant indirection, the de rigueur flattery, of chivalric communication. It is marked by inappropriate garrulousness: Points are made not just once but several times. She is not only setting conditions; she is reminding the English of her king's legitimacy and of the superior moral and spiritual position of her side. She is asserting herself not only as chief of war (a position that had not been given her by anyone in power) but as the emissary of God, the voice of the divine voice.

The letter is astonishing for its naïveté, for its implied expectations. Did she really believe that Bedford, Suffolk, and Talbot were going to read it and say, "Well, then, I guess we'd better pack it in?"

What can they have made of it? Perhaps they received it with a mixture of outrage and disbelief that accounts for their failing to respond to it at all. After the incident of the miracle of the wind changing, when Joan had the confidence of Dunois and his men and her spirits were high, she was frustrated by the English silence and shouted her challenge at them over the ramparts. They shouted back; there was a war of words during which she was called a "cowgirl."

After she had been taken into Dunois's confidence at Orléans and heard the whole of his strategic plan (which she approved), still frustrated with the English nonresponsiveness, she fired a message, wrapped in a crossbow bolt, into the bastille of Les Tourelles. It said, "Abandon your bastilles, and return to your own land, for if you do not, I shall make such a hahay for you that it will never be forgotten: so I write to you—and I shall not write again. Signed: Jhesu-Maria. Joan the Maid."

Upon receiving it, an Englishman shouted, "Here is the latest news from the whore of Armagnac." Hearing this, Joan burst into tears. Here we see an instance of a surprising conjunction: Often, like an overtired child, Joan's boastfulness collapses into tears. This collapse is some indication of her equivocal relationship to being a warrior: She challenges her enemies aggressively, then weeps when they are less than polite. Often the sight of her enemies suffering makes her cry. These two tendencies—boastfulness and tearfulness—come together in a story about Joan and the English captain Glasdale.

Glasdale was one of the Englishmen who had responded to Joan's challenges by calling her a whore. When he was trying to escape from Joan's attack of Les Tourelles, she screamed after him, "Clasdas, Clasdas, surrender to the king of heaven! You called me a whore, but I am sorry for your soul and your men's."[10] Echoing the incident with the guard at Chinon, the drawbridge over which Glasdale and his men were escaping collapsed, and they fell into the river and drowned. Joan's chaplain reported that she wept.

Joan's tears, rather than weakening her, as they have done modern women, seem to underscore her innocence; they become the objective correlative of her virginity; they are a physical manifestation of her specialness. They prove she's still a girl. Perhaps they cleanse the stain of her boastfulness. Girls aren't supposed to brag; they are supposed to cry. Joan's boastfulness and tears, like the outline of her breasts beneath her armor, serve to mark the inescapable duality of her position.

The Girl Among the Boys

From the beginning, despite the outrageousness of her plans, Joan was good at finding men to help her. First there was her godfather, Durand Laxault, then Baudricourt, and the two who joined her at Vaucouleurs, Jean de Metz and Bertrand de Pouligny. There is her mysterious connection with Gilles de Rais, Bluebeard, who joined her at Chinon but dropped out of her life after the coronation. But it was with three soldiers that she made the most satisfying of her friendships. All three—La Hire, Alençon, and Dunois, the Bastard of Orléans—shared her qualities of physical courage, daring, and rashness.

We have seen how Dunois treated Joan with a mix of tact and awe. But their relationship remained professional. Joan's feelings for Alençon were much warmer.

Jean, duke of Alençon, was one of Joan's earliest supporters at Chinon. Joan seems to have been drawn to him from the first. He elicited in her what Edward Lucie-Smith calls her strain of "boastful graciousness." Soon after meeting him, she began showing off for him; she wanted him to know how good she was on horseback and with a lance. He was impressed, like an athletic boy finding out that the girl next door has a good curveball. Like Joan, he had an appetite for war and for adventure, and he allied himself with her very soon after meeting her.

She enjoyed his company, and that of his wife, who was the daughter of her great hero Charles, duke of Orléans. The duchess was worried that her husband would be in danger, having just been released from five years in an English prison. Joan promised the pretty royal wife that her pretty royal husband—Joan always called him her "beau duc"—would be kept safe. And indeed she did, in a way that had aspects of magic to it, later save his life.

Joan had no hesitation or unease at being in the company of this young royal couple. And they, it seems, had no hesitation in accepting her. It is pleasant to imagine this healthy young threesome, eating, walking, joking; with Alençon and his wife, we get a rare glimpse of Joan at ease, a pal, with nothing at stake, relaxing with people who like her.

Her relationship with the soldier of fortune La Hire evokes another kind of glamour. La Hire was given his name either because of his legendary anger (as in Ire) or because he was lamed by a chimneypiece that fell upon him when he was sleeping. He was well known for his ruthless ferocity, his violent temper, his foul mouth, and his laxity in religious observation.

Joan and La Hire were together at Orléans, and in her company he never swore. Once, before he met Joan, when told he had to confess before a battle, he said there was no time, it was essential to attack the enemy promptly. He was prepared to confess simply that he had done "all that men of war were accustomed to do." The chaplain was forced to accept this and gave the absolution required. His penitent thereupon prayed: "God I pray thee that thou wilt do for La Hire as much as thou would wish La Hire to do for thee, if he were God, and thou werst La Hire."[11] When he returned to Chinon after the disastrous Battle of the Herrings (shortly before Joan's entry onto the scene), he found Charles trying to relieve his depression with feasts and leisure. He said to the king, "Sire, I never saw a prince who more joyously lost what was his than you." Although he was a tough campaigner, he was also a dandy; he had made for himself a scarlet cloak covered over with little silver bells, which would announce his movements with their music.[12]

· · ·

Joan's connection with La Hire put her on the side of war-loving soldiers; the one with Alençon and Orléans tied her to the party of the princes of the blood. This put her in radical opposition to the king's cash cow and chief adviser, de la Trémoille, and weakened her bond with Charles and with the group pressing for a diplomatic, rather than a military, solution to the conflicts with both England and Burgundy. She paid a price for her friendship with her three comrades: What did their friendship with her cost them?

It is tempting, and the unsuccessful renderings of Joan on film do it again and again, to paint these friendships in the romantic tonality of boy and girl pals. The appeal is obvious: males and females in harmony, with none of the anxieties or complications of sexual desire. Brother and sister, arm in arm, forgetful of the two-backed beast.

All three of the men were proud of their lack of sexual desire for Joan, although Alençon speaks of the beauty of her body. This is typical of this kind of relationship, in which the girl has no possibility of ever becoming a woman; she is allowed to inhabit the world of action without danger to her chastity; she becomes one of the boys. And the boys, in their turn, stop whorin' and cursin' and drinkin' in her presence. Their wives try to feminize her, but she won't be one of the girls. Not even for a minute. She likes their attention, but she's eager to be off and running, and the wife's job is to stay at home and wait.

The biographies of Joan's three associates are darker than the romance would allow. La Hire was, like many professional soldiers, one of the *écorcheurs,* or fleecers, who had tormented Joan's childhood. Marina Warner describes him as spending a lifetime "marauding on either side of the narrow path between brigandry and soldiering." She recounts a story of his returning the hospitality of a Burgundian duke by throwing him in a dungeon and holding him there until a ransom, a horse, and a quantity of wine had been made over to him.

Even her *"beau duc"* Alençon has some shady moments. Two months after testifying on Joan's behalf at her rehabilitation trial in 1456, he was put in prison for treachery, having supported Louis the dauphin against his father, Charles VII. There was no reason to do this except for the grossest immediate personal gain. The person who arrested him and put him in prison was none other than the Bastard of Orléans, called Bastard no longer but now the lord of Dunois.

Two myths are shattered by the realities of the behavior of Joan's companions. The first is the myth of ennobling influence. Their contact with Joan did nothing to stop Bluebeard from being a murderer of women and children, or La Hire from being a marauder. In addition, there is the myth of soldierly devotion. If it were to have crossed over into life, Joan's friends would have rescued her, or she would have died surrounded by them, beatifically smiling up at their weather-beaten faces, now softened by tears. But they didn't rescue her. They didn't even try to ransom her. When she died, she was alone; her gallant companions-at-arms were nowhere to be found.

CHAPTER V

ACCUSED

WHEN JOAN ENTERED the courtroom at Rouen for the first time in November 1430, she was still young. Six months later, when she was taken from the tower to the stake, she knew she was about to lose her life. But she had already lost something else: her youth.

She entered the trial full of confidence that, accompanied by her voices and the righteousness of her cause, she would prevail. The trial taught her that there were forces stronger than she. The French word for trial is *procès*, and Joan's was, indeed, a process, a process of maturity and loss. In the course of it, she learned her limits. When the nineteen-year-old Joan was led in fetters to the market-place, surrounded by the jeers of a taunting crowd, she was no longer a girl.

Attempts at Escape

Joan had hardly arrived at the fortress of Beaulieu, where she was brought by John, the duke of Luxembourg, before she made her first attempt to escape, prizing up the wooden boards of the floor. In doing this, she raised an important chivalric question and exposed once again her imperfect and uneven relationship to the chivalric code. She claimed not to have given her *parole,* or her word, when she was captured. If she had, it would have meant that she was on her honor not to escape. She said that she refused to surrender on the grounds that she had "sworn and given her oath to someone other than you, and I will keep my word."[1] This is the first instance of Joan's vexed relationship to the issue of oath-taking, her insistence on the primacy of her private relationship to God that took precedence over her responsibility as a citizen or a member of the civil community. In addition to her notion of herself as a visionary, or one in communication with the divine, she was formed importantly by her peasant identity. When accused of bad faith in trying to escape, she replied with the commonsense proverb "God helps those who help themselves." Once again, she was inspired by one part of the knight's identity—the man of action, the man of battle, the man who relieves suffering and creates change; but she was impatient with the parts of the identity that interfered with action and change. After having denied that she had given her *parole,* she brushed off its importance by saying she "forgot" whether she gave it or not and that it was the right of all prisoners to escape and if she had another chance she'd do it again. Simply, she would rather die than be imprisoned. No abstract ideal softened the clarity of that understanding.

Joan's determination to escape wasn't deterred by having been caught. After she was moved to another of the duke of Luxembourg's strongholds, the château of Beaurevoir, she performed one of the most rash and desperate acts of her rash career. She leaped from the window of the castle, a drop of sixty or seventy feet. She was knocked unconscious but sustained only bruises. This is another proof of Joan's incredible health, strength, and powers of recuperation. It could also be another instance of her youthful belief that she could take great risks and not be hurt by them.

Much was made of this leap in the trial that followed, for good reason. Most obviously, it could have been interpreted as a suicide attempt, a serious mortal sin, an automatic guarantee of the soul's damnation, an act that required the witness of the community in forbidding the suicide burial in consecrated ground.

In terms of heroic definition, or self-definition, the leap from the tower is at best an equivocal gesture. The straightforward chivalric hero would not try to escape in this way; he would endure, or he would be rescued, gallantly. Joan's leap is the stuff of peasant comedy: the miscalculation, the stunned rise from the ground. It is cartoonish rather than grand. You can almost see the stars around her head, the tweeting birds representing her concussion. There is something ignominious about her having to be helped up and carried back to the tower; there is something foolish in the image of her bandaged head, the fettered prisoner who might look as if she had just come from the dentist or a barroom brawl.

Joan acknowledged that she did wrong in her leap, but she did it with her usual "That was then and this is now" matter-of-factness. The judges returned to it repeatedly during her trial, and of course they were right to. It was importantly connected to their dual task: determining her guilt and tarnishing her reputation. Part of her defense, or explanation (for she didn't really defend herself, admitting always that the jump was a mistake), was that she tried to escape because she was desperate to be at the side of the people of Compiègne, to protect them in their dangerous hour. "She had heard it said that the people of Compiègne, all up to the age of seven years, were to be put to fire and sword; and that she would rather die than live after such a destruction of good people. . . . She knew she had been sold to the English and she would rather die than be in the hands of the English."[2] Thus, to her mind her leap was a chivalric act; she ignored the risk to herself in the service of aiding the weak who needed her.

The incident of the tower is one of the areas where Joan was a bit slippery about her relationship to her voices. She admitted that she jumped against the advice of her voices, although she tried to wiggle out of admitting that she disobeyed them. Then she said she obtained forgiveness from her voices and was saved from injury and death because of their intervention. Her assertion that she was forgiven by them directly, without her having needed to receive absolution by sacramental means, through the authority of a priest, was an example of the kind of heretical presumption that maddened Joan's judges, that they rightly saw as an assault on the primacy of ecclesiastical authority.

She was unclear about whether or not she thought a leap from a sixty-foot-high tower might result in her death. At one point she said she knew it might but that death would be preferable to being a prisoner of the English. Like many adolescents, the notion of her own mortality seemed not particularly real to her. Her focus was on escaping and getting back to battle. Other people might die when they fell sixty feet, but she would get to Compiègne and, more importantly, get away.

Waiting: The Prosecution

By the time her trial actually began, Joan had been kept a prisoner for eight months. Part of the reason for this is the complications that arose from several groups' vying for the chance to determine Joan's fate. The duke of Burgundy's interests were represented by John of Luxembourg, and his ambivalence about giving Joan up to the English rather than keeping her in Burgundian custody might account for the relatively long time it took the Burgundians to hand her over. He probably thought that he was in a good position to drive a hard bargain, playing the English off against Charles and the French. It would have been expected that an offer would be made for her ransom, for this was the most common course when important prisoners were taken. But the dauphin, whom she made king, didn't lift a finger to help her. Eventually, she was sold to the English for ten thousand pounds, with no counteroffers.

Enter Cauchon

Another group that had a stake in Joan's fate was the officials of the University of Paris. These men were strongly Anglo-Burgundian in sympathy. Two days after Joan's capture, they wrote to the duke of Burgundy demanding that she be given over to them for trial. The man who was chosen by the university to press its claim was Pierre Cauchon, the bishop of Beauvais, who has gone down in history as the villain who engineered Joan's destruction.

Cauchon's scrupulosity was another reason why it took so long for Joan's trial to begin. He insisted that the structure of the trial be impeccable; he said to one of the notaries that he wanted to make a beautiful trial of this: "*unum pulchrum processum.*" Despite his claims, the trial, from the beginning, had an important irregularity. Cauchon would be conducting both the initial interrogation and the trial, and there would be no secular hearing.

Joan was unlucky in her opponent; he was intelligent, well connected, and convinced that he was doing God's work. His type is not unknown: W. H. Auden describes him in his poem "Horae Canonicae." He speaks of such a judge who

> from a glance at the jury . . .
> knows the defendant will hang . . .

[the] lips and the lines around them
relax, assuming an expression

not of simple pleasure at getting
their own sweet way but satisfaction

at being right, an incarnation
of *Fortitudo, Justicia, Nous.*

He goes on to say that

without these judicial mouths

(which belong for the most part
to very great scoundrels)

. . . .

. . . there would be no authority
to command this death.[3]

Cauchon's zeal in prosecuting Joan has, from the beginning, a whiff of the phobic about it. One of the assessors at the trial who was sympathetic to Joan reports that after Cauchon had been sent to fetch Joan from the duke of Luxembourg, he reported the details of his encounter to the duke of Warwick, who represented the British in Rouen, "with joy and exultation." He was not the natural first choice to be in charge of her case; he had to ask for the job. One reason for his ardor is that he lost his see at Rheims to the dauphinists. Bedford tried to make this up to him by having him transferred to Rouen, but the Rouen chapter rejected him because of his high-handedness. He had a reputation for being brilliant but immoderate, as the tone of his letter insisting that the dukes of Burgundy and Luxembourg give her up and his insistence on delivering the letter personally indicate. He would trust the final removal of Joan from Arras to Rouen to no one else—an unnecessary vigilance that hints at a zeal motivated by something other than a mere sense of duty.

He asserted that it was his responsibility to try Joan, since she had been captured in his diocese, but canonically speaking, this was stretching things. Canon law said that Joan could be tried for heresy only in the diocese where she was born or had committed the crime. His prejudice and the irregularities that this prejudice allowed, or encouraged, in him served as the bases for the overturning of his decision at the time of the rehabilitation trial twenty-five years after Joan's death.

The man who was to be in charge of Joan's judicial fate was prejudiced against her on many grounds. He had always been Anglo-Burgundian in sympathy: He had lost his power base as a result of the dauphin's coronation in the city over which he had jurisdiction. He was a favorite of the University of Paris, which was set against Joan not only because of her loyalty to the king but because of her model of authority—mystical, individualistic, female—that was in radical opposition to everything they stood for.

Joan was tried not as a political prisoner or as a traitor but as a heretic. The terms were always religious, and the form of the trial was that of an Inquisition. No specific charges were brought against her in the beginning. Rather, she was questioned in the hope that she might, in the process of the questioning, be brought to admit to some offense, the same method that the Communists used in their show trials. Then the replies would be formulated into articles, which she could refute.

Cauchon's bullying nature asserted itself when he had to include a representative of the Inquisition. The vice inquisitor, Jean LeMaitre, questioned his own competence to serve. But he fell victim to Cauchon's pressure and asserted at the rehabilitation trial that he had been only a reluctant participant and had acted out of fear. Some other clerics were more courageous, and they were punished for their independent stands. Nicholas de Houppeviulle, a theologian, opposed Cauchon, questioned his authority to serve as judge; imprisoned for his importunity, he was released only through the intervention of an archbishop. Another feared for his safety and took off for Rome, where he spent the rest of his life. A third pretended he was drunk when he objected; he was let off with verbal censure.

Cauchon was a formalist; he loved the form and took pride in his adherence to its lineaments, his obedience to its demands. It was necessary that he appoint the required officials, the most important of whom was called "the promoter." In our terms he was the prosecutor. Cauchon named Jean d'Estivet, who had served as his canon at Beauvais. D'Estivet was especially noted for his ferocity and partisanship. He was notorious in his dislike of Joan and for his foul mouth, which was so offensive that even Warwick was shocked. At one point, he disguised himself as a friendly priest and visited her in her cell. It was he, even more than Cauchon, who baited and taunted Joan, and even more than Cauchon, he felt the edge of her sharp tongue.

By the time he was ready to begin, Cauchon had assembled one cardinal, six bishops, thirty-two doctors of theology, sixteen bachelors of theology, seven doctors of medicine, and one hundred other clerical associates. Joan had no one on her side but herself.

It would appear that the procedure was proper, but there was never any possible outcome for the trial except the one that happened. Cauchon would see to that.

Before the trial could take place, the prosecution had to examine witnesses from the prisoner's past life. Cauchon sent representatives to Domrémy, but their replies were so uniformly noncondemnatory (to the point of boredom) that they were not introduced into the trial hearing.

The Trial Begins

During the eight months that she was a prisoner, Joan was guarded by English soldiers, who delighted in taunting her and threatening her chastity. She was chained to her bed. She was refused the sacraments.

From the first day, she entered the courtroom bravely, the youngest, the only female. For all she knew they were, to a man, her enemies; she could not have known which faces might conceal a friendly demeanor. Yet she was fearless, and considering her devoutness, her lack of concern about defying the power of the Church is astonishing. She was defying not only the king of England but the King of Heaven. That, however, was defining things on their terms. On her terms, despite the judges' insistence that she understand the difference between the Church triumphant (the church in heaven) and the Church militant (the church on earth), she believed they did not represent either. They represented the English, the Burgundians. They were just another group of godons. She repeatedly told them that if they brought her case before the pope, she would tell him everything. Cases of smaller import than hers had been brought before the pope, but she was told this was impossible; the pope was too far away. In fact, the assessors knew that the pope would not respond to Joan for fear of alienating the English and their allies. She continued to interpret the body before which she was tried, therefore, not as the Church but as her enemies.

Each day she was escorted from her cell, where she was fettered to her bed, restrained by leg irons. She objected to such treatment; she was told that since she had a record of escape, she couldn't be trusted without fetters. They had, of course, a point.

But how torturing it must have been for this young, healthy animal, who loved movement above all things, to be confined to a dark cell and to a bed within it. Her spirits seemed, however, extraordinarily undampened. She appeared to enjoy the game of question-and-answer and the spectacle of confounding the judges. Although we have many references to Joan's crying, no one reports a single tear shed either in her cell or under the pressure of the interrogation. Her plainspoken, tenacious even-mindedness, her verbal and physical assertion of health, and the fact that self-pity never seemed to occur to her make her a touching victim. She is young and inexperienced; her ardor checkmates their power, and her simplicity confounds their subtlety.

Joan's conflict with her judges began right away, when she refused to take an oath in terms that were satisfactory to them. They adjured her to "tell the truth concerning the things which would be asked her, as much for the shortening of her trial as for the unburdening of her conscience, without subterfuge or craft," and that she should "swear on the holy Gospels to tell the truth concerning everything she should be asked." To this Joan replied: "I do not know on what you may wish to question me. Perhaps you may ask such things as I will not answer." About the secrets she revealed to Charles the king, she at first said they could "cut her head off, she will not reveal them." Then she temporized: In eight days she would know if she ought to reveal them.[4]

Joan was always clear that she was being tried by her enemies, and she believed that because of this she had no responsibility to tell them the truth. From the very beginning of the trial she acted in a way that short-circuited the very assumptions that make trials possible: She would not swear to tell the truth. How can we imagine what she must have imagined the outcome of such resistance might be? Did she think Cauchon and his examiners would say, "Well, of course, we understand very well that you will not tell us everything. Nevertheless, we will proceed along the lines you will lay out"? Or did she think she would be rescued, by the dauphin, by the duke of Orléans, by some of her comrades-at-arms, and the whole trial would be meaningless, therefore nothing to be taken seriously? From the beginning she said she would not speak to the court about her voices, that she would tell the truth in all matters asked her concerning the faith, that she would tell her parents' name and her place of birth. When told to say the Pater Noster, she refused unless Cauchon agreed to hear her confession. He refused. Cauchon was checkmated: He appeared to be withholding the condition—the lawful administration of the sacrament—that would allow things to proceed.

Her refusal to take the oath led to a procedural debate among the judges as to whether she was, in effect, in contempt of court and should therefore be condemned immediately or whether her refusal to take the oath was a tacit admission of guilt on all the charges. What could have been more frustrating to the man who wanted "a beautiful trial" than a girl who refused to take the first step so that the dance might properly begin?

The Charges: Heretic, Apostate, Sorceress, Idolater, Cross-Dresser

Joan was tried by an ecclesiastical court, and so the charges made against her were all religious in their nature. One way of thinking of Joan's hearing is that it was the first of the great witchcraft trials. The fear of witches was entering the European air at the end of the fourteenth century, and it was connected to anxieties about class and particularly gender mobility. By connecting Joan's military victories with witchcraft, the English were able to justify their losses—all the more humiliating, since they were losses to a woman.

This explains the judges' emphasis on the details of folk customs around Domrémy that could be connected to witchcraft. They asked her over and over about the fairy tree and the oak wood, reported to be enchanted, named in the prophecy of Merlin. Joan responded to them offhandedly, as if they were bringing up an old memory, a dim one. She brushed off the prophecy of Merlin, which she referred to when she was trying to convince Baudricourt and the king: something she'd heard of, but that hasn't much to do with her. "I put no faith in it," she said.[5] When the charges were condensed from seventy to twelve, the ones involving sorcery disappeared.

But the ones involving heresy stayed with her, literally to her death. Joan was made to wear the terms of her accusation; she was led through Rouen wearing a shift and a hat, which looked like a dunce cap, upon which had been inscribed the words "Heretic, Apostate, Relapsed, Idolater." The first three charges, which involve her relationship to Church doctrine, make straightforward sense in the historical moment of Joan's life.

But the hat said: Heretic, Apostate, Relapsed, Idolater. The most complicated and interesting of the charges was idolatry.

Idolatry was an elastic, all-purpose charge, and it questioned the mysterious human power to represent and to make images. Tertullian named it "the chief crime of mankind, the supreme guilt of the world, the entire case put before judgment: for every sin is committed within idolatry." Aquinas said: "It was the cause, beginning and goal of every sin because there is no kind of wickedness which idolatry does not produce at some time." The historian Carlos M. N. Eire says, "Idolatry is a fighting word; it presupposes a definition of what is true and false in religion, for an idol cannot universally be recognized as such. . . . One man's devotion was another man's idolatry."[6] Idolatry was one of the three default-settings for medieval accusation, the other two being sodomy and usury. Any of the three of them was flexible enough and wide enough in its applications to ensnare any number of sinners and name as sins any number of hard-to-categorize acts.

The center of the sin of idolatry is its deliberate confusion of category and identity. The sacred image becomes an idol when the perceiver misunderstands its purpose— that of drawing the perceiver closer to the invisible God—

and becomes stuck in the physical properties of the picture or statue itself. Thus it becomes valued in itself rather than as a vehicle to bring the soul closer to the divine. Ideally, the sacred image should eventually disappear in the perceiver's mind; it should melt away, lose its corporeality. If the image disappears, it is, in Aquinas's terms, an example of a "true lie," as opposed to a "fictitious lie," where the form supersedes the function.

Joan was accused of idolatry in connection with two of her most characteristic acts: her relationship to her voices and her wearing of men's clothes. The insistent demand for physical details about the saints to whom she spoke was a way of trying to get her to overphysicalize her saints and turn them from spirits to demons. Or idols. If Joan could be made to say that she experienced her voices not only aurally but by touching and smelling them, she would be committing the sin of idolatry, a deliberate mistake in categorization. She would have failed to allow her voices to return to their proper realm of impalpable orality. She would have made a fetish of them rather than allowing them to become air.

The charge of idolatrous transvestism appears more than thirty times in the trial's text. One charge accuses her not only of wearing male dress but of cutting her hair "like a young fop," pointing out that her doublet was fastened by twenty points and that she wore long leggings laced on the outside, a short mantel reaching to her knees, a close-cut cap, tight-fitting boots, and buskins. She was taking the place not only of a man but of a knight—and a dandy.

In connecting Joan's cross-dressing to the sin of idolatry, the judges were accusing Joan of making an idol of herself. In this, they were taking a rather sophisticated approach, arguing rationally as scholastics rather than appealing to biblical authority. They had to prove that her cross-dressing was of the forbidden rather than the tolerated kind. Not all transvestism was frowned on by Church authority; there is a tradition of "holy transvestites," women who passed themselves off as men in order to preserve their virginity. The details of some of their biographies have unavoidably comic touches. Take the case of St. Margaret, a.k.a. Pelagius, which comes to us from a thirteenth-century collection of saints' lives, *The Golden Legend,* by Jacobus de Voraigne. Margaret decided on her wedding night that she couldn't bear giving up her virginity, so she escaped the bridal bed and betook herself to a monastery, where she passed herself off as Brother Pelagius. She was rewarded for her exemplary conduct by becoming the chaplain at a convent. But enemies accused her/him of impregnating one of the nuns. She allowed herself to be exiled to a cave rather than reveal her secret, which was made manifest only at her death.

Another holy transvestite was St. Uncumber, originally named Willevirgis. The daughter of the king of Portugal, she refused to marry the king of Sicily and prayed that God would allow her to preserve her vow of virginity. Whereupon she was blessed with the gift of a beard and mustache and became St. Uncumber, the patroness of un-

happy wives who wished to be unencumbered of their hus-
bands.

But sanctioned transvestism escaped the accusation of
idolatry because the woman's female identity became invisible, subsumed in the task that the disguise was meant to
effect. She became, to the world, entirely male, not drawing
attention to herself but disappearing into the job of making herself safe from male desire. Joan never passed as a
man. Her cross-dressing made her femaleness a contradic-
tion rather than an erasure; in taking on the power and authority of men, she refused to give up the identity of a
woman.

Questioned as to whether she wanted a woman's dress, Joan
answered in a way that is hard to make clear sense of. "If
you give me permission, give me one, and I will take it and
go. Otherwise no. I am content with this one, since it is
God's will that I wear it."[7] Could she have meant to say, It's
God will for me to dress as I am, that is as a man, but if
you tell me not to, I will disobey God's will if you agree to
let me go? The same ambiguity occurred when she was
asked if the voice had ordered her to wear men's dress. She
answered, "Dress is but a small matter," but said that she
had not "taken it by the advice of any living man."[8]

Most often, when she talked about why she wouldn't
give up male dress, she explained that it was because in female dress she was afraid for her chastity. It is as if, bearing
the sign of a female, she was subject to a female's vulnera-

bilities; signed as male, she was safe. Like her virginity, this seems to be a pact in which both Joan and her enemies agree to a definition of bodily terms that is about the idea of the body rather than its existence in space.

The importance of Joan's chastity to her idea of herself must be measured by her protection of it at the expense of receiving the sacraments. She was, for her time, unusually devoted to the Eucharist; she received great sustenance from receiving Communion and from hearing Mass. At a time when she would have been more than ever in need of spiritual consolation, she forwent it rather than take the risk of sexual violation. Her faith that God would claim her as his own was unshakable enough for her to risk displeasing him by refusing the sacraments; her faith in the stability of her own identity if she lost her virginity was far less secure.

Asked which she would rather do, wear a woman's dress and hear mass or continue in her man's clothing and not hear mass, she engaged in a tricky dance:

"Promise me that I may hear Mass if I wear a woman's dress, and then I will answer you."

She was promised.

She then responded, "And what do you say, if I have sworn and promised our King not to put off these clothes? Nevertheless, I say, Make me a long dress, right down to the ground, without a train, and give it to me to go to Mass and then when I come back I will put on the clothes I now have."

She was told that she must give up male clothes unconditionally.

She replied: "Bring me a dress like that of a citizen's daughter; that is, a long houppelande, and I will wear it, and also a woman's hood, to go and hear Mass."[9]

But she would not agree to wear women's clothes once she had left the chapel and was back in her cell.

What this seems to suggest, although the terms are shifty, is that she didn't object to wearing women's clothing in the safe zone of a church but that she would not wear it in the hostile environment of her cell. What happened after her abjuration, when she agreed in her defeat to put on women's clothes, seems to support her instinct for self-preservation. There are two stories, one by Martin Ladvenu, her confessor, and one by the usher Massieu. They conflict, but they both support Joan's notion that her chastity was dependent on her cross-dressing.

Joan was dressed in women's clothing, but a parcel of men's clothing was left at the foot of her bed. She told Ladvenu that one of her guards tried to rape her and that was why she put on men's clothing again. Massieu's story is that the guards pulled her female clothes off her, kept them from her, and gave her no choice when she was forced to get up to answer "a demand of nature" but to wear men's clothes again or be naked. Whichever story is true, the presence of male clothing in her cell is a puzzle. Was the clothing left there to tempt her, a temptation that her judges, understanding the importance of male dress to her, well understood she wouldn't be able to resist?

The same ambivalence about dress occurs when Joan begs her judges to grant her the grace of a woman's dress and a hood for her head if she is to die. When she's asked why she wants a woman's dress for her last hours, she answers, "It suffices that it be long."[10] As if the issue were not gender but modesty.

A moment later, she says that if they let her go in a woman's dress, she'd put on a man's clothing as soon as she was free. And she would "not for anything take the oath that she will not take up arms or wear male dress to do our Lord's will."[11]

It is difficult to get a firm grip on Joan's position in relation to men's clothes. Sometimes it seems that she was only wearing male clothing as a practical measure and that if her judges had allowed her to resume male clothing in the cell when she was in the presence of her hostile guards, she would wear female clothing in order to hear Mass and do so until her death. But she never agreed to appear before her judges in female dress, and she never agreed to give up male dress for good. Sometimes she said that her voices told her to put on male dress, so if she failed to wear it, she would be disobeying them. Sometimes she went so far as to say that the issue of dress was of minor importance. The only thing we can say for certain about Joan's attitude toward male clothing is that it was inconsistent. Perhaps this is because she had a strong desire to wear men's clothing, but the idea would have been so abhorrent in her time that she knew she couldn't speak of it, and may have been unable to acknowledge it, even to herself.

The Language of the Trial

Joan's judges were clerics, the charges against her were doctrinal, and the terms of the trial were ecclesiastical, but her answers escape the formal boundaries of ecclesiastical, juridical language. It often seems that Joan and her judges are literally speaking different languages. But the judges' language turns dead in their mouths, as when they describe themselves as "benevolent and pitying, wishing and determined to proceed in this matter with gentleness and grace to bring her back to the way of faith and salvation."[12] Her words come to us sounding as lively as the day they were spoken. It is the language of youth, a girl's language. But it is also the language of someone with an extremely good memory and a sense of self-preservation. She is talking to keep herself alive. It is innocent language in the sense of being saturated with her conviction of being free of guilt but not of canniness or even a bit of guile.

Unlike her judges, Joan sometimes uses language for play, and she doesn't avoid exaggeration or passionate words. When refusing to speak about her voices, she says that she "will not reveal them save to Charles . . . and if they cut her head off, she would not reveal them."[13] And when asked if the people in her town sided with the Burgundians, she says she knew only one Burgundian: "whose head she would like to see chopped off, that is if it will please God."[14] When asked if St. Michael wears clothes, she said: "Do you think Our Lord has not wherewithal to clothe him?" When, after hearing the previous day's transcript read to her, she discovered that the notary had made a mistake in recording what she had said, she told him that if he does it again she'll "pull his ears."[15] On an important issue, whether she had given or caused to be given money to the man who had taken Franquet d'Arras, whose death was laid at her feet as a brutality, she said, "She is not the master of the mint or the treasurer of France to give him money."[16] She even taunts her persecutor. When asked for details of her vision of St. Michael, she says to Cauchon, "he's told me some things about you, but I'm not going to tell you right now."[17]

When she speaks the words of her prayers for guidance on the manner of dress, a new kind of linguistic intensity enters the record. Her devoutness is made manifest, and its purity enters the courtroom like a red lozenge of stained glass in an opaque window.

> Most sweet Lord, in honour of thy Holy passion, I beseech thee, as thou lovest me, to reveal unto me what I should answer to these churchmen. I well know, as to my dress, by whose command I took it, but I know not how I should leave it off. Wherefore it may please thee to inform me.[18]

Her response to being asked if she is in a state of grace has the bell-like clarity of a soul sure of its own destiny.

She answered: "If I am not, may God put me there; if I am, may He keep me there."[19]

Joan's judges were frustrated by the clarity of her responses, by the unshakability of her faith, by her refusal to place herself in their hierarchy. She never mistook her place in relation to God; He is her supreme authority. The same sureness applied to her sense of her judges: They had no jurisdiction over her. When she was asked what the voices said to her on the morning of February 27, she replied: "They said I should answer you boldly."[20]

Her diction also included proverbs that indicate peasant morality and common sense: "God helps those who help themselves," in defense of her jumping from the tower, and "People have been hung for telling the truth before now," to defend her refusing to tell the judges what they ask.

If we think of the trial as a musical performance, Joan was constantly the only female solo, and she was confronted by a series of more or less interchangeable male singers who could share their part. They could relieve each other, and she had no relief.

No relief. She had two possible modes in which to operate: She had to answer each question as it came along, which required absolute attentiveness at all times, and she had the silence of her cell, unaccompanied and uncomforted, a silence that also required alertness, since she felt under sexual threat by her guards. If one of her judges grew tired of questioning, he would leave off, rest, and give over responsibility to one of his colleagues. She was entirely on her own. At night, the judges had the company of their fellows, good food, rest in a comfortable bed. She had a dark cell, the company of enemies; she slept in fetters. It is remarkable that she kept her composure, her good humor, her health, and her freshness of thought and diction. The source of her strength was her belief that, wherever she was, she was in company far superior to any that her judges might be enjoying. Each morning, therefore, she was ready again to meet her opponents in a battle of words.

Change of Venue: Shift of Tide

Cauchon soon understood that he was losing the battle and that Joan was enjoying the performance aspects of it. So he changed the nature of the performance from a public to a private one. On March 10, three weeks after the trial's first session, he moved the procedure from the courtroom to her cell; after this, Joan's language lost much of its playfulness. She lapsed into half promises and apologies; she got confused. Then, occasionally, she rallied, and the moments when we see again her old assertiveness are more poignant against the background of the equivocal others. In her cell, the girl whose métier was the spectacle, the battle in open air with pennants and standards flying, was reduced to a space of a few feet and the regard of only enemies whose focus was growing narrower and more hostile. In this new situation, the judges sharpened their questions and introduced topics that were difficult for her to answer with an easy heart: her leap from the tower at Beaurevoir, the capture and execution of Franquet d'Arras, and her fighting on a feast of Our Lady.

Two of the lesser charges of which she thought she might be guilty have a comic aspect. One is the matter of the bishop of Senlis's horse, which she took and returned without paying for it, saying that it was a bad nag and not worth the money. She admitted to having done this but then said she really didn't remember and didn't think it was a mortal sin, because she claimed, untruthfully, to have paid, and if he didn't get it, it wasn't her fault. The second moment with a comic touch occurs when she's accused of having told someone who asked her which of the warring popes she should support that, in effect, "she'd get back to him later." She said that she shouldn't have done it, but she did it when she was in a hurry, when her soldiers needed her, on her way out of town.

The issue of fighting on a feast day was more serious. When asked why she attacked Paris on a feast day and questioned as to whether it was something her voices would have urged her to do, she said, "It is good to keep the feasts of Our Lady from beginning to end." She didn't say anything about her not having kept them. Her slipperiness on this point indicates that she knew she did wrong; she herself refused to attack on the feast of the Ascension, but that was when the military tide was in her favor.[21]

The matter of Franquet d'Arras was more serious still. When she was asked "whether taking a man prisoner and holding him to ransom and then putting him to death is not a mortal sin,"[22] she said she'd never done such a thing, then said that he deserved to be put to death and that the ransom was no longer valid because the prisoner she was going to exchange him for was dead. She spoke about it as a peasant would a horse trade; then she became testy when asked if she gave money to the man who had taken Franquet d'Arras prisoner.

The matters of her attempted suicide, her executing a prisoner she had promised to give up for ransom, and her going to battle on a feast day could, even by a sympathetic judge, be considered mortal sins. In waiting until she was worn down by questioning, in presenting her with these troublesome accusations not in the public courtroom but alone in her cell, in bringing up offenses that, unlike the ones of sorcery and heresy, Joan would have cause to worry about (they were, interestingly enough, faults concerned with bodies rather than ideas), the judges knew that they were playing on Joan's vulnerabilities. They were weakening her when she was already weak.

She had no hesitancy about the other crimes against living bodies of which she was accused. She asserted that she had never killed a man and that she loved her banner twenty times more than her sword.

The King's Crown

Joan's most glaring inconsistencies have to do with the nature of the sign that she gave to the king and the way in which this sign was made known to him. For a long time, she refused to give details about the sign, saying that this was one of the things her judges had no right to know: It was between Charles and her. Her first answers about the nature of the sign were vague enough so that she could not be hurt by them. She said that the sign would exist for a thousand years, that it was in the king's treasury but that she would tell him nothing more.

But in the latter interrogations that took place in her cell, she seemed, almost out of exhaustion, to adopt not only the language but her accusers' imagery. They mentioned an angel; she agreed there was an angel. They brought up a crown; she described it. It is the one lie she admitted to, and on the day before her death, she said in her prison, "It was I who brought the message of the crown to my King. I was the angel and there was no other, and the crown was no more than the promise of the king's coronation which I made to him."[23]

Vita Sackville-West and other scholars say that Joan's lie was not really a lie, only a confusion of metaphor for reality. Her effect on Charles was otherworldly; its goodness and power seemed angelic. Why, therefore, should she not name herself the angel? But it seems to me this confusion is a symptom of her exhaustion and one of the first signs of an intermittent series of breakages that would finally lead to her denial of everything she stood for.

In the middle of April, Joan fell ill, probably of food poisoning. The promoter d'Estivet, Joan's most intransigent enemy, went to her cell to visit her, accompanied by several physicians. One asked what was wrong with her, and Joan blamed a carp that had been sent to her by Cauchon. D'Estivet attacked her. He called her a camp follower and said that she had brought her sickness upon herself by eating herrings. When the physicians told the earl of Warwick, who was representing the British interests at the trial, that she should be bled, he advised them to be careful; she was cunning, and he didn't want the bleeding to be an excuse for another suicide attempt. He wanted her death public, and he wanted credit for it.

While she was still weak but recovering, Cauchon visited her in her cell and exhorted her. Her answers to his accusation were among her most despairing, but within two days she rallied again, and when shown the instruments of torture, she said that they could pull her limb from limb and she wouldn't change her story.

Accusation, Condensation, Exhortation, Abjuration

On March 27, Joan was read the seventy articles spelling out her crimes. She was offered counsel but refused it. The judge said, "Joan, my most dearly beloved, it is now time for you to think well about the end of your case and what you have said and done."[24] Putting the judges' position into terms to which Joan the soldier would be most susceptible, he continued: "Think well, Joan: if there had come some knight into the court of your king while you were there, a man of your seignory, saying, I will not obey the king and none of his officers shall make me submit to him, would you not have said he stood condemned?"[25] Joan may have hesitated for a moment, but finally her courage came back: Her king was not Henry VI of England but Christ.

On April 2 the court considered Joan's answers to the seventy articles, and they were compressed to twelve. On April 5, they were submitted to the judges, who were told to give their opinions in writing by the tenth. Only a few did. On April 13, the twelve articles were taken to the University of Paris for consideration. On April 18, Joan was exhorted in prison; on the nineteenth, she was shown the instruments of torture.

After they had been considered for more than a month, Joan was read the articles that had been approved by the university, and she was "charitably admonished" before sentencing. Five days later, she was let outside for the first time in many months, to the cemetery of St. Ouen, where she would be publicly and formally excommunicated. Her head was shaved. She was dressed in women's clothes, the clothing of female penitence. It was the first time since she had begun her career that she appeared in public in women's clothes.

There were three platforms: one for Cauchon and the tribunal, the second for the bishops and clergy from Rouen and its environs, the third for Beaufort, the cardinal of England. There was a high scaffold on which Joan and the preacher would be visible to the crowd. The preacher spoke on the text: "A tree beareth not fruit of itself." During this sermon, Charles VII was attacked, and Joan defiantly shouted: "Do not talk about the king. He is a good Christian. Talk about me."[26] Once again she appealed to the pope, asserting that she would abide by his decision, but her appeal was ignored. It may have caused Cauchon and the other judges to make a last attempt to have her recant, however. The attempt led to a delay, and it made the crowd restless. Some people from the crowd began throwing stones. From where she stood, Joan, could see the executioner with his cart and the materials for the fire.

Suddenly, Joan joined her hands and said that she submitted to the authority of the Church. She prayed to St. Michael for direction. Cauchon turned to Beaufort, the cardinal of England, for advice. As representatives of the spiritual authority of the Church, they had to accept Joan's submission as the outcome they had all along been pressing for. But Warwick, the representative of the English political interests, said they had been too lenient with her; they had let the bird fly away.

There has been a great deal of dispute about the form of abjuration that Joan signed. At the rehabilitation trial, witnesses said that what Joan signed was very short, "the length of a Pater Noster." The document that was presented was considerably longer than that:

I, Joan, called the Maid, a miserable sinner, having now realized the sink of error into which I had come and having by the grace of God returned to holy church our mother, in order that it may be seen I have returned to her not half-heartedly but with a good heart and will, do confess that I have grievously sinned by claiming lyingly that I had revelations from God and his angels St. Catherine and St. Margaret and all those my words and acts which are against the church I do repudiate, wishing to remain in union with the church, never leaving it.[27]

The statement is signed—Joan knew at least how to sign her name—and her signature is followed by a cross. The cross, however, is problematic; it was the sign Joan habitually gave when she meant that what had gone before it should not be believed.[28] One witness observed at the rehabilitation trial that after she had repeated the prescribed formula of abjuration, she laughed. Whether this was nervous laughter or not, whether the cross was a habit or a signal for disbelief, we cannot know. We do know that Joan believed that her abjuration would free her from prison.

The Recantation Recanted

Joan was led back to her cell, shamed and defeated. She had saved her life; she believed she had bought her freedom.

When she entered her cell, she was in women's clothes. The confusing explanations of how she got back into men's clothes cannot be resolved, but it is possible that the very act of putting them on renewed her courage. Or perhaps it finally dawned on her that she would spend the rest of her life in an English prison. She had said before that death was preferable to that, and perhaps the certainty of her understanding of this gave her a moment of exhilaration, and returned her heart and soul. Whatever led to her decision, on May 28, she was back in men's clothing and insisting that she had sinned in abjuring; that she had done what she had done "for fear of the fire" and now she was ready to die.

In two days, she had taken an enormous journey. She had been walked in chains from the cemetery to the prison, having given up all her heroism. She was the victim of some sort of sexual brutality or sexual trickery; either an attempted rape, or a group of louts pulling off her clothes and waiting for her to give up in order to relieve herself. Somehow in that time, she grew into a hero, not in military or spectacular terms, but in spiritual ones. She faced her death calmly, perhaps even with joy. This could have been because she had fully decided that death was preferable to betraying who she was and what her voices had said.

One of the great puzzles of Joan's last days is that Cauchon allowed her to receive Communion. If she was excommunicated, she should have been denied the sacraments. This anomaly was brought up during the rehabilitation trial as a proof that Cauchon knew he was acting in bad faith.

On the thirtieth of May, Joan walked in chains to the marketplace. She was executed by the secular arm of the English government, although her trial was ecclesiastical.

Since the time she had left Vaucouleurs, she had been surrounded by adoring crowds; now a jeering mob lined the
side of the road, clamoring for her death. She walked in silence, barefoot, her head down. When she arrived at the
marketplace and saw the pyre, she wept. She was led up
some stairs to the stake to which she was tied. She asked to
have a crucifix held in front of her, and an English soldier
put together two sticks and gave them to her. Her loyal
confessor, Martin Ladvenu, rushed to the church and
brought a golden crucifix, which he held in front of her
eyes. The fire was lit; soon she was invisible within the
flames.

The executioner reported: "Once in the fire she cried
out more than six times 'Jesus!' and especially in her last
breath she cried with a strong voice 'Jesus!' so that everyone
present could hear it; almost all wept with pity."[29] Her end
was a slow one. The executioners had been told to keep her
a distance from the flames so that the death would be as
difficult as possible.

After Joan died in the fire built for her in the market square
at Rouen, her body, charred, but still recognizable, and still
tied to the stake, was displayed so that the crowd who had
come to see her execution could examine it. They were
looking in order to certify that she was, in fact, female. Our
knowledge of this comes from an enemy of Joan's, the
Bourgeois of Paris, who records it in his journal. The Bourgeois was Burgundian in his sympathies, and intensely crit-
ical of everything having to do with Joan. But his enmity is

short-circuited for a moment by the horrifying spectacle of strolling observers:

"She was soon dead and her clothes all burned. Then the fire was raked back and her naked body shown to all the people and all the secrets that could or should belong to a woman, to take away any doubts from people's minds. When they had stared long enough at her dead body bound to the stake, the executioner got a big fire going again round her poor carcass, which was soon burned, both flesh and bone reduced to ashes."[30]

The Retrial

Eighteen years after Joan's death, on December 10, 1449, Charles VII solemnly entered the city of Rouen. It had been under foreign occupation for thirty years.

Charles had done nothing to help Joan while she was in danger; now, understanding that his authority was importantly tied to her legitimacy, he made it his business to right the wrong, which he was happy to lay exclusively at the feet of his enemies. His own negligence was never mentioned. One of his first acts after his entry to Rouen, however, was to order one of his counselors, Guillaume Bouillé, former rector of the University of Paris, to start an inquiry into what had happened to Joan.

Although Joan had been officially declared a heretic, the people had already begun creating myths about her. Her heart would not burn to ashes; a dove had been seen flying over the pyre, in the direction of France. The city of

Orléans provided for the support of her mother and brothers. It was noted that the three men most responsible for her death met suspicious ends. Cauchon died suddenly while his beard was being trimmed; d'Estivet disappeared mysteriously, and his body was found in a gutter; Nicholas Midi, the inquisitor, was stricken with leprosy.

The year 1450 saw many dramatic events. The English king was rapidly losing Normandy. Nicholas V, elected pope in 1447, was a strong leader who was able to restore order to the papacy. He was sympathetic to Charles because Charles had supported him against the antipopes. The party of the University of Paris, Joan's enemies, had been on the other side, the side of the Council of Basel, which opted for a weaker papacy and a stronger episcopate.

It was during this year that Charles appointed Guillaume Bouillé to investigate Joan's trial. He was as sympathetic to Joan's cause as Cauchon had been hostile. He called only seven witnesses; the first was Guillaume Machon, the notary who had taken down the proceedings and had, even at the time of the first trial, noted irregularities. There were two Dominicans, Martin Ladvenu and Isambert de la Pierre, who had been sympathetic to Joan in her last days. There were rumors that Ladvenu had tried to signal his advice to her during the trial. He had been her confessor, and de la Pierre had ministered to her. Two other priests, Guillaume Duval and Jean Toutmouile, had been present at some hearings; the latter had accompanied Ladvenu when he gave Joan the last sacraments. Jean Massieu, who had accompanied Joan from her cell to the trial, was called. He had been twice sentenced for doubtful behavior having no connection to Joan; it was he who had allowed her to look into the chapel for a glimpse at the altar on her way from her cell to the courtroom.

The only truly hostile witness was Jean Beaupère, who had been one of Joan's fiercest antagonists, and to whom Joan had made her famous answer about being in the state of grace. He was unrepentant and pitiless toward her, telling the examiners that "she was very subtle with a woman's subtlety."[31] His obvious spite did his case no good.

The result of the inquiry was brought to the king in letters under cover and seal. The inquiry found the trial prejudicial to the point where it should be counted void. But the king had no power to undo the official trial. His inquiry had no real weight; Joan had been tried by the Inquisition, and only the Inquisition could vindicate her.

In August 1451, the pope sent his legate to Charles. He was shocked by Charles's coldness and reluctance. It would appear that although Charles knew it was inevitable, he was uncomfortable with the Inquisition's having asserted its authority in a way over which he had no power. Nevertheless, it was in his interest to have an official rehabilitation trial set in place, and the inquiry opened in 1452. The examiners drew up an official questionnaire; they would have to examine far more than the seven witnesses the king's inquiry had called. Three years elapsed between the findings of this hearing and the pope's order that the procedures be officially begun. But the pope had had other distractions. In July 1453, Constantinople fell to the Turks. At this time, the Eastern and Roman branches of the Church were attempting to work together to defeat the Turkish enemy. But the attempts failed. Understandably, Joan's hearing held a low priority for the pope, but after a three-year delay, the official hearing began, in November 1455.

In a move designed to play on the popular sentiment that surrounded Joan, the pope's legate arranged that the case be introduced by Joan's mother, Isabelle Romée. Isabelle was of very advanced age and was brought out of years of retirement in Orléans to confront the learned doctors, this time in the Cathedral of Notre-Dame de Paris. Like her daughter, female and illiterate, she confronted the all-male assembly. Unlike her daughter, however, she was flocked by supporters and well-wishers. The crowd was carried on waves of emotion when she repeated her petition:

By my legal marriage, I brought into the world a daughter whom I duly caused to receive the honour of the sacraments of baptism and confirmation, whom I brought up in the fear of God, respectful and faithful towards the Church insofar as her age and the simplicity of her estate allowed. . . . Then, although she had not thought, or plotted or done anything not according to the faith . . . envious persons wishing her evil . . . embroiled her in an ecclesiastical trial . . . wickedly condemning her at the last and burning her.[32]

Unlike her daughter's, Isabelle's words proceeded from someone else, learned doctors and lawyers who used their learning to help rather than undo her.

After Isabelle presented her petition, she fell to the ground in a faint.

This Mater Dolorosa raises an interesting issue about Joan. Of all the images that have been created about her, there is none that takes away our surprise that she was someone with a mother.

Like the original trial, this one was limited by the concepts and language of the judicial form. And like the first trial, it was formally impeccable and entirely biased. The bias this time was in Joan's direction. What was proved was that the first trial was improper and prejudiced. Its inconsistencies and irregularities were pointed out: Joan should have been held in an ecclesiastical, not a secular, prison; she should have been given a secular trial before she was executed by the state. Cauchon's sincerity was called into question, and his decision to allow Joan to receive Communion was cited as evidence that he knew she was innocent; otherwise, he would have been participating in a sin of sacrilege. The witnesses to Joan's childhood in Domrémy, whose testimony had been suppressed in the original trial, were recalled.

Questions that would have put Joan in a bad light were now passed over, the very ones that were emphasized in the original trial. Joan's cross-dressing was never mentioned. Her voices were deemed authentic because "every word of them testifies to the most devout piety . . . she had very good reason to trust in her voices, for in very truth she was delivered, as they promised, from the prison of the body by martyrdom and a great victory; the victory of patience."[33] This is, to say the least, a defense that skirts the difficult issues of inspiration and its verification. If death can be interpreted as delivery, then we will all be delivered.

Joan's refusal to obey the duly established arm of the Church is glossed over; she is said to be pious and loyal; it is asserted that no one explained to her the difference between the Church triumphant and the Church militant, which is demonstrably untrue.

In July 1456, the documents of Joan's original trial—the articles of condemnation and the sentence—were burned formally and publicly in Rouen, in the *Vieux Marche*, the very spot where Joan had been executed.

A directive was given that no images or epitaphs to Joan be set up at Rouen or elsewhere. The directive was ignored.

Two years later, Isabelle Romée died in Orléans.

CHAPTER VI

VIRGIN BODY

Postmortem

THE DISPLAY of Joan's charred body to gawking passersby in Rouen ranks high in the annals of brutal exposure. It is impossible to imagine a male hero for whom such display would be required as a proof of any kind of authenticity.

Of all the offenses heaped on Joan, this posthumous one is arguably the cruelest. Her virginity was one of the most important ways that she knew herself. Her transvestism, which was one of the major accusations leveled against her, was something she took on in large part to prevent herself from being looked at as a woman and to protect herself from the vulnerability that could follow upon such looking. The integrity of her body was of primary importance to her, an integrity for which virginity was a metonymic part, if not the whole story. Her horror at being burned arose because it was, for her, an unclean death. One of her last statements was a cry of outrage about the manner of her death: "Alas! Am I so horribly and cruelly used, that my clean body, never yet defiled, must this day be burnt and turn to ashes! Ha! Ha! I would rather be beheaded seven times than suffer burning."[1] It is not the

painfulness of the death that appalls her but its unclean-
ness, its "defilement," as if the consumption by flames that
would be the mode of her death had, for her, a sexual
component. She would be devoured, and above all, she had
wished to be intact: recognizable as whole.

The Narrative of Joan's Virginity

Perhaps the only thing that Joan and her accusers agreed
upon wholeheartedly was the importance of her virginity.
They agreed on its importance, but did they agree upon its
meaning? What, in fact, did it mean?

It is difficult to define the meaning of something whose
distinction is the refusal of participation, a willed lack of experience, an insistence upon not joining in one of the species'
major projects, a state whose national anthem is "no."

What is the "no" a resistance to, and what does the resistance buy? In our age, when the consequences of loss of
virginity are slight, it requires an effort of imagination to
understand the importance of virginity in the past both literally, as a means of safeguarding life and health, and sec-
ondarily, as the only possible hope a woman had of
autonomy. Until very recently in the history of the world,
it was unlikely that a woman would make a mark or a name
for herself in any place outside the traditional roles of
wife, mistress, or mother; for her to break free from those
roles, she had to be untouched, literally, by the phallus, but
also by its associations. It was only by refraining from the
most easily understood avenues to pleasure and fleshly

connection that the possibility of autonomy could, however tentatively, exist.

At its least potent, virginity was the minimum condition for a woman entering a traditionally male sphere; at its most powerful, it invested its possessor with an aura that traveled between the sacred, the mystical, and the magical. Joan understood this well, and so did her accusers.

The first recorded act that involves the preservation of her virginity was also her first conflict with both parental authority and the law. In 1428 she was involved in a breach-of-promise suit. A young man claimed that she had promised to marry him and then reneged. This means that she must have been pledged to a young man, probably by her father, and her refusal to carry through the commitment had to be adjudicated by a civil court. It was only the first of four trials with which she was associated, two of which—her rehabilitation and canonization trials—took place after her death.

But a breach-of-promise trial was, it seems, an appropriate beginning to her public career, and not only the litigious aspects of it. She had to stand up in court for the right to refuse the normal lot of women, and perhaps—if we believe that she did once consent to marry the young man or at least didn't oppose the prospect—she had to stand up for the right to change her mind. Either way we understand the case, it is a portent of the shape of the rest of her public history. Either she was misinterpreted (she did not consent to the marriage but was perceived to have consented), or she shifted her ground. Because both are characteristic of later events, either interpretation is possible. But the area of contention in the breach-of-promise suit is the intersection of her fate with her bodily life, more particularly its sexual aspects.

We know from this case that Joan fought against relinquishing her virginity by invoking the law. And we know that her explanation for adopting the clothes of men—one of the aspects of her behavior that was most challenging to her accusers because it broke the unwritten law of sexual custom—was that it safeguarded her in a life lived among men. What it safeguarded was her virginity. It prevented her from being an object of male desire. Her companions in battle prided themselves on not feeling desire for her—all the time asserting their virility in other circumstances, suggesting that their lack of desire for her was a proof of the sacred character of their knightly manhood and of her specifically female magic.

Not for the first time, her short-circuiting the normal sexual path was seen as positive, a source of power.

A puzzling factor in the treatment of Joan by her enemies after she was taken prisoner is their collusion in the agreement that her virginity was, if not sacred, at least something deserving of honor. Considering the cruelty of their treatment of her—she was fettered, deprived of light, air, and movement, deprived of the sacraments, verbally in-

sulted and taunted, shown the instruments of physical torture, perhaps even poisoned—it is remarkable that her
guards, all male, all her sworn enemies, should have refrained from raping her. In the last, worst phase of her imprisonment, she complained that she was threatened with
rape, but the threat was not carried out.

The situation of Joan's imprisonment included many
elements of torture; it is surprising, therefore, that her enemies refrained from using one of the oldest methods of
torture practiced on women prisoners. It would have been
easy for one of her guards to have raped her and denied it.
Her virginity, her magic, would have been shattered, and it
would have been her word against that of her accusers. In
the climate of disbelief that was growing up around her
when things started going badly for her in the last days of
her trial, when the sense of her power was radically dimin-
ished, why would her protestations of rape have been taken
seriously? People were already doubting the authenticity of
her voices, suggesting that they might be either demonic or
invented. Why would it be any more difficult to cast doubt
on the veracity of her reports of violation? Many women
have been disbelieved when they have told their accounts of
rape. It is in the interest of a male-dominated sensibility to
suggest that rape is a female fantasy. What was it about
Joan that kept her enemies from using what would have
been their last, best weapon against her?

Joan's virginity was constantly subject to tests, to which
Joan willingly submitted. (Her willingness to submit to
these tests was later counted against her by the devil's ad-

vocate who argued against her canonization.) But the tests seem almost pro forma, as if the outcome were already known and the procedure only a formal covering of bases. As Marina Warner has noted, the tests were far from scientific. Joan was examined most frequently by nonprofessionals, well-born women whose names, rather than their skill or experience, were what qualified them to make judgments. What were these women looking for, how did they look, and how did they know what they had found? One of the women who attests to her virginity makes her assertion after having seen Joan entering the bath. This same woman says that Joan's extensive horseback riding had resulted in her behind being completely covered in calluses. If what constitutes a definitive proof of virginity is an intact hymen, wouldn't the same extensive horseback riding that had covered her in calluses have broken her hymen?

How is it possible to explain the force of the idea of Joan's virginity? What was it that allowed the very men who calmly discussed whether or not to use the instruments of torture that would break her bones and pull her limbs from their sockets to be on Joan's side when it came to the protection of the thing about her that was more important to her than her life? What made them say: "This far and no further?" Why were they free to shackle her body, to burn it, and yet compelled to preserve a bodily distinction that was, after all, invisible to them? Was the sacredness of her virginity so immediately comprehensible to them that it overrode their hatred? This is a psychological anomaly, another sign of the singularity Joan was able to claim for herself and that most of the women in the history of the world have not been granted. What was it about her that made men want to destroy her body but keep her image—based crucially on a bodily state—intact? How do we explain Joan's power to create a narrative whose subject is her body, a narrative so compelling that her enemies fell under its sway? Could it be that Joan's enemies feared her even more than they hated her and that the seat of their fear was Joan's virgin body? If so, they would have been fetishistically afraid to violate the site of their fear, whereas acting out their hatred on parts of her body other than the fetish site—her limbs, for example—might have served as something of a relief. And burning the virgin body would have immolated the threat: Having been devoured entirely, the body could not rise up and devour them.

It is not possible to speak about Joan of Arc without keeping in mind that every act of hers was performed by a female body, a virginal one. Because most people in the history of the world have believed that important public acts are performed by a male body, one that is sexually experienced with partners whose identity and number are irrelevant, no investigation into a male hero's sexual behavior—unless he were suspected of homosexuality and therefore of having some of the qualities of a woman—would be required. Nor would its marking be important in our understanding of a male hero. Minus a hymen, what might such a mark be?

Everything Joan did was colored by the accident of her femaleness, like a foreign accent that inflects every syllable and determines the interpretation of every word. We would respond to a man with Joan's career in a way so different from the way in which we respond to her that it would be unrecognizable.

The Rest of Joan's Body

Joan's femaleness was the most important thing we understand about her body and its meaning to us, but what did Joan's body mean to her? In which ways was it a source of pleasure and pride to her? In which ways a cause of anxiety and mortification?

We know about the importance of her virginity to her. We know, as well, that she didn't care much about food. Those around her were impressed by her abstemiousness at table. Even after the most strenuous battles, she was known to eat only a few pieces of bread dipped in wine. Like her chastity, her lack of appetite for food was seen as an indication of her worthiness or fineness or superiority. It would have been unbearable that a woman of appetite either be given authority by men or be allowed to live among them. The lightness of Joan's physical desires was the quality that allowed her, for a time, not to overbalance the fragile craft made up of men's phobias about woman and their idealization of her.

Although Joan didn't care much about food, she was drawn to luxurious and elaborate clothing. To be sure, it was the elaborate clothing of a man, more particularly a knight. Her judges accused her of dressing "like a young fop," thereby crossing not only gender but class lines. One of the ironies of her capture is that she was pulled off her horse by her fancy cloth-of-gold jacket. Had she been dressed more simply, she would have been harder to unseat.

We know that Joan had beautiful breasts because several men—her squire and her closest companion-at-arms—mentioned them. But of all her boasting of qualities and accomplishments, she never mentioned the beauty of her form as something of which she was proud. When a tailor tried to touch her breasts during a fitting, she laid him flat on his back.

We have information about Joan's breasts, and this reminds us of the centrality of the sexual female body to everything having to do with her life. It is unlikely that we would know the details of any of the sexual characteristics of a male hero. We don't know, for instance, the size of Napoleon's penis, although in its mummified state it was auctioned at a great price and is now in the possession of a New York physician, a collector of curiosities. Joan's breasts, however, were thought a proper topic for discussion even at her rehabilitation trial. Or only at her rehabilitation trial, as though they were somehow important in creating a good image of her. At the trial that resulted in her death, where everything introduced was meant to make her look bad, her breasts were not mentioned.

Joan took pleasure in her body not as an eating body or a body that aroused or experienced sexual desires but as a body that wore clothes and used them for display, as a body that rode horses and was admired on horseback, as an active body that led men and wielded a sword. The traditional capacities of the female body never, it seems, were of much interest to her. She was never a man's lover and never bore a child. We have reports that she was kind to children and that they were drawn to her, but no mention on her part of any longing for maternity.

It was customary for single women to sleep beside other women for safety, and Joan's page reports that she much preferred sleeping beside young rather than old women. But whether this has sexual implications or simply indicates a wish to be with someone close to her own age is a matter of speculation.

We also have testimony from her page concerning Joan and one of the other common properties of the female body. Joan did not menstruate. Her page would have known this, because he was in charge of the care of her clothing.

Amenorrhea is a well-known phenomenon among women athletes; it also accompanies anorexia—and Joan's reluctance to eat more than the minimum needed for survival suggests that she might not have been taking in the proper number of calories to encourage menstruation. The combination of extreme physical activity, extreme stress, and a minimum of food easily explains Joan's not menstruating. But once again she is placed, or she places herself, apart from the common lot of women.

.   .   .

When Joan has been depicted visually, most frequently she is slender and blond. But contemporary reports tell us that she was dark, stocky, and short in stature, so short in fact that she had to be provided with a block in order to easily mount her horse. Except, that is, when she was performing the cowboy trick of landing on her horse's back from a running jump.

Whatever the reality of contemporary witnesses, however, the dominant northern aesthetic since the Renaissance requires slimness and fineness, and in its iconic demands on Joan the culture has insisted that she take on the properties of its most common dreams.

The sexual allure of boyishness attaches not to strength but to lightness. But Joan was not an English public school boy; she was a tough peasant girl. Her skeleton was not long and thin in structure. Perhaps Bastien-Lepage's muscular dreamer gives something of the quality of Joan's peasant physicality, but I'm not sure. His Joan is a rustic beauty. People who spoke of Joan's physical appearance stressed health and strength and vigor. And lovely breasts. But no one speaks of her as having a lovely face except for those who see her from a distance of centuries, a figure not of history but of longing. For them she is the girl/boy saint, untouched, immaculate, a creature not of earth but air. In fact, her body mirrors both her language and her actions. Joan was down-to-earth. In her career as a soldier and a servant of the king, this would be her undoing. In her posthumous career as a saint, she was stripped of gravitas in order that she might be well and easily beloved.

Postparade

After her body was exposed and examined by passersby, it was returned to the fire, where it was burned to ashes. These were thrown into the Seine to prevent the cultivation of relics. It is said, however, that no matter how long it was left in the flame, her heart could not be consumed. Of the fate of Joan's unconsumable heart, we have no word.

CHAPTER VII

FOOD FOR THE FEAST

SHE HAS BEEN RE-CREATED by more writers who can readily be called great than any other figure: Shakespeare, Voltaire, Schiller, De Quincey, Twain, Brecht, Shaw. This list excludes the merely good, among whom I would place Anatole France. Many mediocre films have been made about her and one great one. Even Jesus has not fared as well; perhaps only Napoleon has come close.

The writers who have made something of Joan have provided a feast that we in the West have continuously consumed. They have taken what they needed of her, a clutch of chefs searching out markets for the tenderest ingredients to create succulent meals that will show off their talents and their tastes, rejecting or ignoring what will not serve either. These meals are in no way to be mourned. Indeed, the variety of the dishes simply marks the richness of what Joan suggests, the variousness of our needs for her or for some pure girl who entered the larger world and gave her life for it.

That masterpieces have been created with Joan as their subject is undeniable; that none of them has presented her in her radical contradictions is undeniable as well. But artists' choices are based on what suits their gifts and their convictions about what is important in the world. The writers who have made Joan their subject have needed her for their own reasons, just like French nationalists or devout Catholics or girls wanting to leave home. In the end, however, it doesn't matter how much of the historical Joan gets into the play, the poem, the film. It succeeds or fails on the basis of whether or not its language creates vivid images. The terms are the same whether we are talking about Joan of Arc or Madame Bovary.

Dreyer and Shaw

The two greatest works having to do with Joan both center importantly on Joan's trial. Yet if Dreyer's Joan and Shaw's Joan were to meet leaving the courtroom, they wouldn't recognize each other. It is as if each man had agreed to ignore the part of Joan that the other had so beautifully treated.

The Passion of Joan of Arc, which was made in 1928 by the Danish director Carl Dreyer, is, in the words of one critic, the greatest film about suffering ever made. Indeed, its title necessarily calls to mind the Passion of Christ. Dreyer said of it, "I wanted to interpret a hymn to the triumph of the soul over life."[1] The film's technique is dependent on close-ups. Dreyer's Joan, played by the Italian actress Maria Falconetti, is not only a tragic figure; she is a pathetic one, pathetic in the deepest sense, a sense that has nothing in it of condescension. The obsessive attentiveness of Dreyer's camera allows no distance between the viewer and Falconetti: Our hearts must break along with hers because she is young, and pure, and ardent, and she will be overmastered by the dried-up and vicious old men who are her judges. She weeps tears that might well be tears of blood, like Jesus in the Garden. Her death is not only a triumph; it is—for her and for us—a welcome relief.

Falconetti's agonized face, a face of a beautiful, anguished, but still-healthy young woman, is juxtaposed against the wizened, hate-filled faces of her judges and the horrifyingly gross and vacant faces of the crowds, like the spectators at one of Van der Goes's crucifixions. The austerity of the film's technique—the movement between faces, the sparseness of the setting (a bare cell, an official courtroom), the symbols that are invoked to indicate Joan's visions (the shadow of a cross, a skull, a crucifix against a smoke-filled sky), the very slowness of its movement—gives it the hypnotic quality of dream, or rather, the liminal zone between dream and waking.

The film's greatness would be impossible without the nuances created by Falconetti, who was nearly psychologically destroyed by Dreyer's demands on her in the course of the film. She never made another film, and her daughter wrote a bitter book about her mother's fate at the director's hands. Dreyer found her in a Paris boulevard theater: "She was playing there in a light modern comedy and she was very elegant in it, a bit giddy but charming."[2]

There is certainly no hint of the giddy, or even the superficially charming, in Falconetti's Joan. This is Joan after she has been defeated; ostensibly, the film covers the whole trial, but none of Joan's sprightly, impatient give-and-take with her judges is suggested. She has been overmastered by the gravity of her situation, by its hopelessness and deprivations, from the first moment we see her on the screen. She is a transcendent victim, but a victim nonetheless. Nothing suggests that she has the slightest impulse to help herself or to resist her fate.

Conversely, Shaw's Joan seems to suffer for less than twenty-five lines in a 125-page script. She is a sturdy Yorkshire lass with no doubts, no equivocations, no one she can't outtalk. Like all of Shaw's heroes, she is dauntless and hyperarticulate. We meet her when she convinces Baudricourt, by her sheer high spirits, to outfit her. She moves to confront the dauphin, whom she addresses as "Charlie" and whose effete malaise she overcomes because she seems to offer him a kind of maternal protection from the bullies who surround him.

Shaw's Joan, first played by the triumphantly earthbound Sybil Thorndike, is religious only because her creator, in feeling he has to be true to history, cannot make her otherwise. His unease with this aspect of her leads him to some marvelous leaps and sallies, particularly in his preface, which, as is the case with so much of Shaw, is at least as interesting as the play itself. Shaw was fond of presenting himself as a man of paradox, if not perversity, and this leads him to portray Joan's persecutor, Cauchon, as a just man who was standing up for what he believed in and tried to create as fair a trial as he could. Shaw also defends the Catholic Church as at least as intellectually respectable as modern science and pseudoscience. This leads to some fancy philosophical cartwheels to explain Joan's voices, to which he is sympathetic but in whose literal truth, he hastens to reassure us, he cannot believe. He explains them, at one point in the preface, by calling Joan a "Galtonic visualizer": "Joan was what Francis Galton and other modern investigators of human faculty call a visualizer. She saw imaginary saints just as some other people see imaginary diagrams and landscapes with numbers dotted about them and are thereby able to perform feats of memory and arithmetic impossible to nonvisualizers."[3]

At times, he seems to understand the strength of her faith, the depth of her attachment to the sacraments. The priest who held the cross for her so she could see it at the moment of her death says: "When I had to snatch the cross from her sight, she looked up to heaven. And I do not believe that the heavens were empty. I firmly believe that the Savior appeared to her then in His tenderest glory. She called to him and died. This is not the end for her, but the beginning."[4] Yet he is much more comfortable with a position she reverts to, that she was a girl of great intelligence and common sense. When Baudricourt tells her that her voices come from her imagination, she says, "Of course. That is how the messages of God come to us."[5] And during her trial she says (contrary to the facts) that her voices are always right "even if they are only the echoes of my own common sense."[6]

The vitality of Joan's language carries the play along;

Joan is not a complicated character; she experiences almost no conflict except for the few moments when she takes back her recantation because she understands that she is being offered not freedom but life imprisonment. In her evocation of animal joy in the natural world, we fully experience the poignance of her choice.

> You promised me life but you lied. . . . You think that life is nothing but not being stone dead. It is not the bread and water I fear; I can live on bread: when have I asked for more. . . . Bread has no sorrow for me, and water no affliction. But to shut me from the light of the sky and the sight of the fields and flowers; to chain my feet so that I can never again ride with the soldiers nor climb the hills; to make me breathe foul damp darkness, and keep me from everything that brings me back to the love of God when your wickedness and foolishness tempt me to hate him; all this is worse than the furnace in the Bible that was heated seven times.[7]

But she returns after death in the play's epilogue, cheerful, undeterred by having been burned. She forgives all her enemies and humorously contemplates the spectacle of herself as a canonized saint. Almost to the end, Shaw remains a Shavian. When Joan suggests that she try for the miracle of bringing herself back to life, all the characters—Dunois, Charles, Cauchon—who have just finished expressing their reverence for her, are horrified at the thought. The soldier who presented her with the two sticks in the form of a cross to hold in her bosom and who in return is given one day a year off from hell, which he says is as dull as "a wet Sunday,"[8] must return to his infernal residence just before the curtain comes down. The play ends not wittily but poignantly, with Joan declaring, "O God that madest this beautiful earth, when will it be ready to receive Thy saints? How long, O Lord, how long?"[9]

Brecht and Péguy

The press of the world shaped the idea of Joan for Brecht and Péguy in a way that it did not for Shaw and Dreyer. It would seem at first that there would be little similarity between Bertolt Brecht, the creator of the alienation effect and supporter of Marxist revolutionary violence, and Charles Péguy, the romantic Catholic socialist who advocated communitarianism based on the spirit of the Gospels. Yet both created a Joan who is moved primarily by her overwhelming response to the plight of the helpless victims of the larger social disorder and the effects of violence upon the lives of the poor.

And in both their dramas, Brecht's *Saint Joan of the Stockyards* and Péguy's *Mystery of the Charity of Joan of Arc*, the public or ritual aspects of drama are employed. Brecht invokes street music, and Péguy the litanies and chants of Christian rite, but both aim for a drama that is not out of touch with its communal roots. For both of them see in Joan a type: the martyr for the cause of the people. Of course, their ideas about what can and should be done for the people are radically different. One only has to listen to the different tonalities of the titles of their works—*Saint Joan of the Stockyards, Mystery of the Charity of Joan of Arc*—to feel the difference. Yet both see in Joan one who hungers and thirsts after justice and will not be satisfied on this earth.

Charles Péguy wrote about Joan again and again. This is not surprising, as he was a native of Orléans, scene of Joan's greatest triumphs and the seat of her cult. But Joan's claim on Péguy was not a mere matter of geographic accident. Its roots were historical. For Péguy came to political maturity as a result of the Dreyfus case. He was the only prominent Catholic thinker to support Dreyfus, and he estranged many of his natural religious allies by taking this position. Originally a supporter of Jean Jaurès, the socialist leader, he broke with him later as a result of Jaurès's anticlericalism. Péguy's relationship with the official Catholic Church was vexed; the right-wing authoritarian cast of the French Church in his time appalled him, and he was public and vocal in his criticism of it, as it was in its criticism of him. And yet his vision of a better world was indelibly Catholic and French. The French soil itself was sacred to him, and the ways of rural France conducive to social salvation. Modernization, industrialization, urbanization were the enemies of the spirit; the mystery of the sorrow at the heart of the universe could only be solved for him by the mystery of Christ on the Cross.

So in the same way that Brecht requires indulgence of a contemporary reader—a post-Marxist reader who has seen the Berlin Wall and all that it represented collapse—a reader of Péguy must silence his or her initial resistance to the Romantic Catholicism that forms a basso continuo to his *oeuvre*. Yet the passion for justice that informs both works bathes them in a light that, in its life-or-death quality, compels our attention and our regard.

As Péguy was moved by the Dreyfus case and the injustice that it represented to embrace a program of communal sacrality, Brecht was moved by the economic collapse of Germany in the twenties to see the only possible hope for the poor in revolutionary Communism. In May 1929, the police chief of Berlin had prohibited all demonstrations, and the young Bertolt Brecht saw from a window the breakup by the police of a Communist demonstration, which resulted in the deaths of twenty people. It was in this year that he wrote *Saint Joan of the Stockyards*, a drama set in Chicago. The villain, a megacapitalist named J. Pierpont Mauler, destroys the lives of everyone around him by his unfeeling speculation, even though he claims to be a sensitive man who can't bear the suffering endured by the cattle whose slaughter is required for his potted meat. Joan Dark is a Salvation Army girl, a member of the Black Straw Hat Brigade, who believes in personal salvation for the poor through personal acts of charity and a devotion to the Gospels. In the end, Joan gives this up for a Marxist philosophy, saying, with regret for her collaboration with the oppressors, "Take care that when you leave the world you were not only good but are leaving a good world."[10]

The play is dramatically uneven; Marxist clichés ("The Communists turned out to be right. The masses shouldn't have broken ranks"[11]) are mixed with moments of piercing emotional insight. In Brecht's version of Joan's recantation, she wants to abandon the poor to go back to middle-class safety. Here she speaks of physical realities that the strikers must endure:

> It wasn't this cold in my dream. When I
> came here with great plans, fortified
> by dreams, I didn't dream that it could be so cold
>   here.
> Now what I miss most of all
> is that warm scarf of mine. You people here
> may well go hungry, you have nothing to eat
> but for me they're waiting with a bowl of soup.
> You may well be cold
> but I can go any time
> into the warm room
> pick up the flag and beat the drum and talk
> of Him who has His dwelling in the clouds
> I choke with fear
> of this not eating, not sleeping, not knowing what
>   to do
> habitual hunger, humiliating cold,
> and above all, wanting to go away.[12]

But, like the original Joan, she recants her recantation and dies to bear witness to the capitalist oppression of the poor. For she has understood that without the necessities of life there can be no goodness, no spiritual value, no humanity worth speaking of at all. She defends Mauler's victims when he calls them subhuman. She takes the part of the woman who agrees to keep quiet, in exchange for twenty free lunches, about the fact that her husband fell into the bacon maker; of the boy who takes the husband's coat in return for his silence and a job; of the tin cutter who lost an arm and who doesn't warn Joan, when she pretends to be his successor on a dare from Mauler, of the dangers of his job.

> Certainly she would have liked
> to be true to her husband as others are.
> But the price was too high: it came to twenty meals.
> And would the young man on whom
> any scoundrel can rely
> have shown the coat to the dead man's wife
> if things had been up to him? . . .
> If their wickedness has no limits, their poverty
> has none either. Not the wickedness of the poor
> have you shown me, but
> *the poverty of the poor.*[13]

There is an echo of this deep sympathy for the plight of the poor radically transformed, yet audible, in Péguy's *Mystery of the Charity of Joan of Arc.* Joan, despairing, prays for understanding for the sufferings of the poor as a result of the war. Joan says to her friend Hauviette:

Just now I saw two children on their own coming down the path over that way; the big one was dragging the other along; they were crying and calling out: I want something to eat, I want something to eat. . . . I heard them from here. I gave them what bread I'd got, my food for midday and for four o'clock. They fell on it as if they were animals; and them being as glad as they were made me sick, because suddenly, in spite of me, something got through my head. I saw something, and I thought of all the others who are starving and who get nothing to eat, of all those in misery who get no comfort. I thought of the worst off of all, those who come last, those who are really cast off, those who don't want to be comforted, who don't want anything any more; how do you give to somebody who doesn't want to receive anything any more? I felt that I was going to cry. Then I turned my head away because I didn't want to make them upset, the two children there.[14]

Hauviette, Joan's friend, is a commonsensical girl: You do what you can, she says to Joan, you feed whom you can, and while they're eating, they're happy. But she senses that Joan can't be comforted by her middle-range solution. "You are hungry for other people who are hungry, even when they aren't hungry,"[15] she says.

The other character in this three-character play is Sister Gervaise, a contemplative nun who has retreated from the wickedness of the world in order to pray for it. Her solution is also impossible for Joan, who must try to act in order to save everyone. She doesn't listen to Sister Gervaise's accusations of her lack of humility: Even Jesus understood that he couldn't save Judas, Sister Gervaise says to her. They part, understanding that their ways are dissimilar: Joan must save everyone, not feed one child at a time or pray for one soul at a time. She must act to transform the world. For Brecht, this transformation can happen only through Marxist revolution; for Péguy it can occur only through a kind of mystical French nationalism that will disinfect the land of its corruption.

There is no psychologizing in *Saint Joan of the Stockyards,* whereas Péguy's play is an extended examination of conscience in which not the psyche but the soul is formed. This is achieved in a highly repetitive, poetically hypnotic prose that has a monochrome somberness whose tonality is similar to Dreyer's film.

The slow, repetitive movement of Péguy's style could not be more different from the trudge and swing of Brecht's, and yet both are shot through with a cry of anguish: What is to be done with the suffering of the poor?

Brecht and Péguy share another characteristic in their portrayal of Joan. Unlike every other artist I can think of who has chosen Joan as a subject, gender is, for both Brecht and Péguy, largely irrelevant.

Shakespeare, Schiller, Verdi

This was not true of Shakespeare, Schiller, and Verdi, for whom Joan's femaleness, and especially her virginity, were at the center of their dramatic portrayal. Each of these three giants failed to create a successful portrait of Joan, and each failure is particularly nationalistic in its tone. The grossness of the national traits betrayed in each work gives them the flavor of caricature, almost like a nightclub comedian doing his impression of the Englishman, the German, the Italian.

Shakespeare's *Henry VI* may not even have been by Shakespeare. It may be a product of his tinkering with the work of his inferiors, something he did to hone his craft (or maybe just earn money) while he learned it. Shakespeare's Joan is not only a slut but a witch; her sorcery is the only possible explanation for British defeat at the hands of the militarily inferior and generally spineless French. Every imaginable anti-French cliché is tossed into the pit—along with every assumption about a woman who makes a place for herself in the world of men. Not for a minute are the doughty English taken in by the wench: They know her for what she is. In an exhibition worthy of the Elizabethan equivalent of a junior-high playwriting competition, Talbot, who is portrayed as a cross between Charlemagne and Jesus Christ, shows impatience with the French lingo. When he hears of the dauphin and La Pucelle, he says, "Pucelle or pussel. Dolphin or dogfish / Your hearts I'll stamp out with my horse's heels." (I.4.107–108) (A puzel was a slut; a dogfish, the sea's most unworthy catch.) In a penultimate scene that doesn't rank among Shakespeare's immortal moments, Joan, threatened with death by burning, asserts that she is pregnant. First she names the dauphin as the father, and then, seeing that this only encourages the English to destroy the potential heir, switches the paternity to Alençon. When he is called by Richard Plantagenet "that notorious Machiavel" and his issue considered worthy of death, she tries again with the king of Naples. To which Warwick replies in an excess of pre-Victorian prudery, "A married man! That's most intolerable." (5.4.78) Seeing that her ploy is in vain, Joan goes off to the stake cursing her executioners with a vivacity of language that prefigures later greatness: "May never glorious sun reflex his beams / Upon the country where you make abode; / But darkness and the gloomy shade of death / Environ you, till mischief and despair / drive you to break your necks and hang yourselves." (5.4.86–90)

If you find this Joan hard to recognize, try the High Romantic German version by Schiller. Like Shakespeare, Schiller finds Joan's virginity a problem, but he's not aggressive toward the idea of Joan as virgin, just regretful at the waste implied. Every man who gets close to Schiller's Joan falls in love with her and is inspired not with lustful thoughts but with marital ones. Dunois and Alençon vie with each other over who deserves her more. But Joan is impervious to their charms; her spiritual crisis occurs when she meets Lionel, a brave English knight, whom she cannot bring herself to run through with her sword. The sight of his unvisored face leads her to question whether a life of virginity was the right choice for her, and although she flees before even their trembling hands can meet, she accuses herself of bad faith.

Who? I? The image of a man
In my pure bosom deign to carry?
This heart, which Heaven's glow o'erran
Dare it an earthly love now harry?
I, my fatherland's deliveress,
The highest God's protectoress,
For my own country's foe inflamed?
May that to the chaste sun be named,
And I not be destroyed by shame?

Schiller presents us with a series of plot twists that makes soap opera look minimalist. Immediately after the dauphin's coronation, Joan is accused of witchcraft by her father, who never liked the idea of her refusing the local boys. She flees into the forest, accompanied by a shepherd who has loved her (chastely) since she was a girl. She is captured by the English in the forest, put under the charge of King Charles's wicked mother, Isabeau, who sticks a dagger into her skin, and meets up in chains with (guess who?) Lionel, who offers to marry her and take her to England, where she'll be appreciated. This causes her to remember that her true loyalty is to France. She breaks her chains and gallops back into the battle beside the brave dauphin, where she dies, not at the stake but gloriously at the side of her fighting king.

Many of these elements, but Italianed, are present in Giuseppe's Verdi's opera *Giovanna d'Arco*. The libretto, written by Timistocle Solera, includes an irate father who accuses his daughter Giovanna of polluting the family honor by being the lover of the dauphin. But he is wrong, wrong. He has misinterpreted Joan and the dauphin's chaste love. (They met while Charles, meditating in the forest, came upon Joan praying and was struck by her beauty.) But she resisted the temptation of the demonic chorus, who called her ungrateful in wasting the precious gifts of youth and beauty in a foolish devotion to virginity. "You crazy girl. You are lovely, what are you doing? If you lose the flower of love, it will soon die and never return." Her only option, having been driven from her father's home, is to turn to a life of soldiering. She is captured by the English, and her father somehow happens to be in the tower where she is imprisoned. He overhears her in prayer and realizes that he has accused her falsely. He realizes the enormity of his error and begs her forgiveness. The emotion of this reconciliation allows Joan to break her chains and make her way back to the battle, where she dies, protecting both Charles and her father from the enemy. No burned flesh for Schiller or Verdi: only triumphant death in battle, the clean death at the sharp point of a sword.

Hooray for Hollywood

These distortions are small potatoes considering what Hollywood, even some of its best directors, has done to Joan. Otto Preminger's *Joan of Arc*, with a screenplay by Graham Greene, which he tried to disavow, is mainly about Jean Seberg's short haircut. In Victor Fleming's 1948 *Joan of Arc*, Ingrid Bergman does no better; she is all starry-eyed Scandinavian idealism—her performance is utterly wooden. These actresses are too old and too feminine to get the important element of Joan's boyish youthfulness, and the scripts are too clumsy to accommodate her twists and turns. Perhaps the success of Dreyer's script lies in its silence. And certainly the overlong *Joan of Arc* by Jacques Rivette could use a little of Dreyer's stoic simplicity.

Interest in Joan never flags. In the last year of the millennium there were two new films made about Joan of Arc, one for American television. It was advertised as "the $20 million production, featuring an all-star cast, million dollar consumer print campaign, CBS's biggest and most expensive miniseries to date." This is doubtless true. The kindest thing that can be said for it is that the actress playing Joan looks the part, although she delivers her lines with the flatness of a depressed teenager telling her parents she's on the way to the mall. Throughout, Joan seems to be involved in a massive twelve-step program. On the way to Orléans, Dunois says to her, "Joan, you have to take things one day at a time." The young woman who played her told an interviewer that she liked playing Joan "because she was such a good person and I felt playing her made me a better person." The Ukrainian star of another recent Joan film, who posed for *Vanity Fair* wearing a gingham bikini, said in that interview: "Joan was really a mover and a shaker. She was a real Tasmanian devil."

Right. On the other hand, she may be no further off the mark than Shakespeare or Schiller.

CHAPTER VIII

SAINT JOAN

EVEN CENTURIES as the angel of men's imagination did not make it easy for Joan to be named a saint by the Roman Catholic Church. It was in 1869, nearly 350 years after her death, that the process of formal canonization was begun, and she was not declared a saint for another 50 years.

At the same time that her cause was being discussed, the question of Christopher Columbus's sanctity was also up for debate. But his case was dropped in 1892 on the grounds that he had an illegitimate son. This seemed to be an insurmountable problem overcoming the glory that he earned because "he did not hesitate to conquer the dark sea and to thrust himself into every kind of vicissitude in order to acquire new shores for the Gospel and enter into their possession in the name of Jesus Christ."[1] This transformation of Columbus's career as an explorer into one of evangelization indicates the problems for someone like Joan or Columbus, someone whose fame was achieved by exploits not specifically religious in nature. In order to be named a saint, the candidate has to be understood to have been acting for the greater good of the Church and in ways that conformed to the Gospel. As with Columbus, it required a certain amount of quick-stepping to interpret Joan's goal of uniting France under the scepter of Charles VII as a sacred mission.

That this was done for Joan and not for Columbus points to an aspect of the Church's canonization process that is always present, if not dominant. At any historical moment, the Church canonizes people to make a point about what it considers, at that period, an exemplary life. A saint is not made a saint because canonization does anything for him or her; presumably, he or she has already achieved eternal salvation. A saint is canonized to help the living, and the nature of the help that the living need is often determined by the contemporary pressures of the world on the Church.

Although the first and most natural question regarding Joan's canonization is "Why did it take so long?," the more fruitful and interesting ones are "Why did it happen when it did?" Or, "Why did it happen at all?"

The process that resulted in Joan's canonization began in 1869. The France of that period was at the center of the intellectual and social phenomenon that the Church, beginning with Pope Pius IX and continuing to the present papacy, considered one of the greatest threats ever to its power. This was a series of impulses over which the Church spread the linguistic tarpaulin of the word "modernism," a habit of mind that was secular, rationalist, and antihierarchical. Joan's canonization in 1920 can be seen as the Church's attempt to recapture the larger public imagination for itself. It was one response to the tide of socialist, anticlerical thought that was particularly powerful at the end of the First World War. Many in the Church believed that this tide, whose source was clearly in France, could potentially capsize the boat piloted by Peter's heirs to the papacy. What was needed was the ballast of Joan's image: the popular, and unmistakably loyal, daughter of the Church.

There is a certain irony that this loyal daughter of the Church was sentenced to death by an ecclesiastical court, but this irony was passed over for the greater good of a clearly legible symbolic truth. The greater irony is that this woman, who insisted upon the primacy of her individual experience, and has therefore been called by some the first Protestant, would be seen as the curb by which the faithful could be brought to obedient, communal heel.

It was an irony not unregarded by the devil's advocates charged with disproving Joan's qualifications for sanctity. This was only one of the problems that they addressed, and it is difficult not to sympathize with their reservations. In examining Joan's history of resistance to her clerical judges, they questioned whether this constituted a model of faithful obedience, whether, in presenting her for emulation by the faithful, the Church was backing the wrong horse, or filly.

It is important to understand what is in the mind of the Church when it names someone a saint and, in this context, to explore the differences between a saint and a hero. The Church's criteria for sainthood are based on a person's having lived an exceptional, in fact unimpeachable, life of virtue. The emphasis is placed on the three theological and four moral virtues; it is assumed that the candidate would have kept the Ten Commandments of Moses and the six commandments of the Church—the latter having to do with questions of fidelity to worship. Keeping the commandments is only paying membership dues in the club of potential salvation; it implies only the minimum compliance (however rare that might be in reality), not the distinction that sainthood implies.

The three theological virtues are faith, hope, and charity; the four moral virtues are prudence, justice, fortitude, and temperance. Whereas none of her devil's advocates question whether Joan was an admirable and heroic person, they assert again and again that she was imperfect in her practice of the virtues.

Of all those who have tried to understand Joan's life and career, it is only the devil's advocates who have focused in a concerted way on Joan's inconsistencies and erratic behavior. None of them suggests that she is not remarkable, but they note her radical shifts. They bring up several events in her life that they determine as less than saintly. Some of their objections are easy to dismiss. They accuse her of disobedience to her parents in not telling them about her voices; they fault the perfection of her chastity because of her boasting about it and her willingness to undergo physical examinations to verify it. They are worried that so many different men seem to have mentioned, and therefore seen, her breasts. They charge her with intractableness in refusing to answer the judges at her trial, ignoring the fact that this was her judicial right.

More serious for Joan's admirers, they insist that her throwing herself out of a seven-story tower was an act either of attempted suicide or presumption or, at best, a lack of submission to her unjust judges, thereby refusing the example of Jesus. They note that she lied by her own admission about the details of an angel bringing the king's crown. They suggest that her voices might have been the result of a hysterical delusion and remark that even correct prophecy isn't indicative of the holiness of the visions. They cite the case of Savonarola.

They question her faith and her fortitude, saying that these were present only when things were going well for her. They understand that she was badly treated by those who condemned her (some of the consultors use this as an argument against proceeding with Joan's case, since it will only air the Church's historical dirty laundry), but they contend that her desire to escape from prison, the complaints with which she received her sentence of death, her tears and dread when she was brought to the stake, although understandable and even poignant in human terms, are evidence that she did not possess saintly fortitude.

They repeatedly assert that because of her stubborn refusal to submit the questions of her voices' validity to the Church fathers who were judging her, she is not a model for the faithful. They question whether she isn't just a military or a nationalist hero. One consultor wonders whether, since France has been such a source of poisonous ideas and so much trouble to the Church, maybe her cause wasn't a good one. Wouldn't the Church, he suggests, have been better off if France had ceased to exist? They say that she is different from the Old Testament heroines—Judith and Esther—with whom she was compared, because their works were a direct preparation for the coming of Christ, whereas hers were only rooted in the fate of one country.

Most importantly, they say that she is not a martyr. They repeat the evidence that she did not want to die, that she in fact tried to prevent her death, particularly by her abjuration. They compare her to the earlier Christian martyrs, who embraced death and wouldn't have lifted a finger to keep it back. They suggest that had they behaved like Joan, we would have no models of perfect martyrdom.

But Pope Pius X and the College of Cardinals wanted Joan; they dismissed any negative evidence. Perhaps the true miracle of Joan's canonization is that the Church, in its desire to create a saint who would bring the wandering sheep back into the fold, who would provide a simple and unassailable enough force to counteract the lure of modern pleasure-seeking and free thought, put aside their narrow standards. They forgot their devotion to obedience and conformity and created a saint who is full of contradictions and imperfections that make, if not a saint, then a great and lovable human being. The devil's advocates, unlike the admiring artists who did their part to ensure for Joan a different kind of immortality, understood her changeability and its implications. In this they honored her complexity with a clear gaze, clearer than many of those who loved her for their own reasons.

Their understanding was silenced, and the Church, like everyone else who was to use Joan for his or her own needs, presented us with another oversimplification. But a look at her in the clear light of her words and actions creates an image not of singleness but of fascinating complexity. She was a virgin, and she died for what she believed, but she does not fit the type of the virgin martyr. Ardent, impatient, boastful, resistant, implacable, she is, like all great saints, a personality of genius. Unlike most of the saints, she defined the Church on her terms, not its own.

But what is signified by the word *saint*, and of what use is such a word to those of us who have ceased to believe in the certifying power of a group of men appointed in the name of the Roman Catholic Church? What category of human activity does the word *saint* still meaningfully describe?

Perhaps we should look first at what associations come with the word both to those for whom it is a living term and to those for whom it is a merely recognizable one, denoting something to which they have no access and in which they may have no interest.

"Saint" connects immediately to "goodness." But what does goodness mean to us now? Which are the virtues that we prize? Is it possible for us now to prize any virtue, believing (all of us necessarily post-Darwinian if not post-Freudian) that we act as we do from self-interest?

Is our willingness to still keep the word *saint* in our lexicon a crack in the matte wall of one of our important understandings of the world? Does the word create the possibility, glimpsed, and urging a quick discard, of action beyond self-interest? A passionate economy of sheer spending where what needs to be done, what is compelling and desirable, all come together for more than isolated moments in a human life? A way of life lived in a radical present tense in which cost is uncalculated and the future someone else's to regard?

Those who have treasured saints have done so because they provide a dream of accompaniment, a hope of advocacy, a special connection based on something particular: shared traits, a profession, a name, a date of birth. In return for devotion, there is the sense of being singled out by the saint or being part of the saint's small elect. The saint is simultaneously folded into the life of the devoted and worn as a cloak and talisman. She provides inspiration. Above all, she is someone to whom the votary bows.

With all these considerations in mind, what kind of saint could Joan be? Not, perhaps, the patroness of France; rather, the patroness of the vivid life, prized not for military victories but for the gift of passionate action taken against ridiculous odds, for the grace of holding nothing back. She was canonized for the wrong reasons, but her words and actions are stronger than the seal set on her by some men in Rome. She leaves behind her a record that, if looked at closely, hops and leaps, moves not in a smooth glissade, but in a series of fits and starts. Perhaps the most fitting tribute we can give her is to acknowledge that any understanding of her will be partial and that so compelling a figure will constantly demand new visions, new revisions. For she inspires in those whom she compels a response that the word *hero* is too distant properly to serve. She asks to be made our own; she speaks to our need, passionate, beyond or prior perhaps to reason, to feel that we are hers.

But she will not stand still for us.

Notes

INTRODUCTION

1. See Shulamith Shahar, *Childhood in the Middle Ages* (London: Routledge, 1990).

CHAPTER 1

1. Régine Pernoud, ed., *Joan of Arc by Herself and Her Witnesses,* trans. Edward Hyams (New York: Scarborough House, 1994), p. 32.
2. Pernoud, p. 20.
3. Edward Lucie-Smith, *Joan of Arc* (New York: W. W. Norton, 1977), p. 75.
4. Elizabeth Alvilda Petroff, ed., *Medieval Women's Visionary Literature* (New York: Oxford University Press, 1986), p. 19.
5. Pernoud, p. 172.
6. Pernoud, p. 188.
7. Pernoud, p. 192.
8. *The English Mail Coach and Other Essays,* ed. Ernest Rhys (London: Everyman Library, 1933), pp. 142–3.
9. Johan Huizinga, "Bernard Shaw's Saint," in *Men and Ideas* (New York: Harper & Row, 1970), p. 222.
10. Karen Sullivan, "I Do Not Name to You the Voice of St. Michael: The Identification of Joan of Arc's Voices," in

Fresh Verdicts on Joan of Arc, ed. Bonnie Wheeler and Charles T. Wood (New York: Garland, 1996) p. 97.

11. Marina Warner, *Joan of Arc: The Image of Female Heroism* (New York: Knopf, 1981), p. 135.

12. Warner, p. 178.

CHAPTER II

1. Edward Lucie-Smith, *Joan of Arc* (New York: W. W. Norton, 1977), pp. 64–5.

2. Lucie-Smith, p. 30.

3. Régine Pernoud, *The Retrial of Joan of Arc: The Evidence at the Trial for Her Rehabilitation, 1450–1456*, trans. J. M. Cohen (New York: Harcourt Brace, 1955), p. 87.

4. Régine Pernoud, ed., *Joan of Arc by Herself and Her Witnesses*, trans. Edward Hyams (New York: Scarborough House, 1994), p. 39.

5. Lucie-Smith, p. 57.

6. Lucie-Smith, p. 59.

7. Lucie-Smith, p. 66.

8. Lucie-Smith, p. 74.

CHAPTER III

1. Régine Pernoud and Marie Véronique Clinì, *Joan of Arc: Her Story*, trans. and rev. Jeremy duQuesnay Adams, ed. Bonnie Wheeler (New York: St. Martin's Press, 1998), pp. 40–41.

2. Edward Lucie-Smith, *Joan of Arc* (New York: W. W. Norton, 1977), p. 150.

3. Lucie-Smith, p. 148.

4. Lucie-Smith, p. 154.

5. Lucie-Smith, p. 155.

6. Lucie-Smith, p. 155.

7. Lucie-Smith, p. 166.

8. Régine Pernoud, ed., *Joan of Arc by Herself and Her Witnesses*, trans. Edward Hyams (New York: Scarborough House, 1994), p. 125.

9. Lucie-Smith, p. 164.

10. Lucie-Smith, p. 166.

CHAPTER IV

1. Vita Sackville-West, *Saint Joan of Arc* (New York: Doubleday, 1991), p. 217.

2. Sackville-West, p. 217.

3. Max Weber, "The Nature of Charismatic Domination," in *Max Weber, Selections in Translation*, ed. W. G. Runciman, trans. E. Matthews (Cambridge: Cambridge University Press, 1978), p. 229.

4. Edward Lucie-Smith, *Joan of Arc* (New York: W. W. Norton, 1977), p. 203.

5. Sackville-West, p. 247.

6. Sackville-West, p. 248.

7. *The Trial of Joan of Arc: Being the Verbatim Report of the Proceedings from the Orléans Manuscript*, trans. and ed. W. S. Scott (London: The Folio Society, 1956), p. 82.

8. Sackville-West, p. 149.

9. Régine Pernoud, ed., *Joan of Arc by Herself and Her Witnesses*, trans. Edward Hyams (New York: Scarborough House, 1994), p. 70–71.

10. John Holland Smith, *Joan of Arc* (London: Sidgwick and Jackson, 1975), p. 68.

11. Lucie-Smith, p. 96.

12. Lucie-Smith, p. 96.

CHAPTER V

1. *The Trial of Joan of Arc: Being the Verbatim Report of the Proceedings from the Orléans Manuscript*, trans. and ed. W. S. Scott (London: The Folio Society, 1956), p. 89.
2. *The Trial of Joan of Arc*, p. 111.
3. *Collected Poems*, ed. Edward Mendelson (New York: Vintage Books, 1991), pp. 631–2.
4. *The Trial of Joan of Arc*, p. 63.
5. *The Trial of Joan of Arc*, p. 76.
6. Quoted by Susan Schibanoff, "Transvestism and Idolatry," in *Fresh Verdicts on Joan of Arc*, ed. Bonnie Wheeler and Charles T. Wood (New York: Garland, 1996), p. 32.
7. *The Trial of Joan of Arc*, p. 76.
8. *The Trial of Joan of Arc*, p. 79.
9. *The Trial of Joan of Arc*, p. 117.
10. *The Trial of Joan of Arc*, p. 118.
11. *The Trial of Joan of Arc*, p. 121.
12. *The Trial of Joan of Arc*, p. 121.
13. John Holland Smith, *Joan of Arc* (London: Sidgwick and Jackson, 1975), p. 152.
14. *The Trial of Joan of Arc*, p. 63.
15. *The Trial of Joan of Arc*, p. 74.
16. *The Trial of Joan of Arc*, p. 88.
17. *The Trial of Joan of Arc*, p. 115.
18. *The Trial of Joan of Arc*, p. 140.
19. *The Trial of Joan of Arc*, p. 73.
20. *The Trial of Joan of Arc*, p. 72.
21. *The Trial of Joan of Arc*, p. 73.
22. *The Trial of Joan of Arc*, p. 111.
23. *The Trial of Joan of Arc*, p. 114.
24. *Joan of Arc in Her Own Words*, comp. and trans. Willard Trask (New York: Books & Co, Turtle Point Press, 1996), p. 143.

25. Holland Smith, p. 101.
26. Edward Lucie-Smith, *Joan of Arc* (New York: W. W. Norton, 1977), p. 265.
27. Holland Smith, p. 165.
28. Lucie-Smith, p. 268.
29. Régine Pernoud and Marie Véronique Clinì, *Joan of Arc: Her Story*, trans. and rev. Jeremy duQuesnay Adams, ed. Bonnie Wheeler (New York: St. Martin's Press, 1998), p. 136.
30. Marina Warner, *Joan of Arc: The Image of Female Heroism* (New York: Knopf, 1981), p. 14.
31. Régine Pernoud, *The Retrial of Joan of Arc: The Evidence at the Trial for Her Rehabilitation, 1450–1456*, trans. J. M. Cohen (New York: Harcourt Brace, 1955), p. 15.
32. Holland Smith, p. 184.
33. Pernoud, *Retrial*, p. 246.

CHAPTER VI

1. *Joan of Arc in Her Own Words*, comp. and trans. Willard Trask (New York: Books & Co, Turtle Point Press, 1996), p. 143.

CHAPTER VII

1. Quoted by Natalie Zemon Davis, "'Any Resemblance to Persons Living or Dead': Film and the Challenge of Authenticity," *Yale Review* 86 (1986–7), p. 466.
2. Mark Nash, *Dreyer* (London: British Film Institute, 1977), p. 53.
3. *Saint Joan*, ed. Dan H. Laurence (London: Penguin, 1989), p. 18.
4. *Saint Joan*, p. 142.
5. *Saint Joan*, p. 59.

6. *Saint Joan,* p. 110.
7. *Saint Joan,* p. 137.
8. *Saint Joan,* p. 152.
9. *Saint Joan,* p. 159.
10. *Saint Joan of the Stockyards,* trans. Frank Jones (Bloomington: Indiana University Press, 1969), p. 120.
11. *Stockyards,* p. 102.
12. *Stockyards,* p. 96.
13. *Stockyards,* p. 51.
14. Péguy, *The Mystery of the Charity of Joan of Arc,* adapted Jean-Paul Lucet, trans. Jeffrey Wainwright (Manchester: Carcanet, 1986), p. 20.
15. Péguy, p. 21.

CHAPTER VIII

1. Quoted by Henry Ansgar Kelly, "Joan of Arc's Last Trial: The Attack of the Devil's Advocates," in *Fresh Verdicts on Joan of Arc,* ed. Bonnie Wheeler and Charles T. Wood (New York: Garland, 1996), p. 206.